Cambridge Elements ≡

Elements in Publishing and Book Culture
edited by
Samantha Rayner
University College London
Leah Tether
University of Bristol

VIRAGO REPRINTS AND MODERN CLASSICS

CLASSICS

The Timely Business of Feminist Publishing

D-M Withers

University of Reading

CAMBRIDGE
UNIVERSITY PRESS

CAMBRIDGE
UNIVERSITY PRESS

University Printing House, Cambridge CB2 8BS, United Kingdom

One Liberty Plaza, 20th Floor, New York, NY 10006, USA

477 Williamstown Road, Port Melbourne, VIC 3207, Australia

314–321, 3rd Floor, Plot 3, Splendor Forum, Jasola District Centre,
New Delhi – 110025, India

79 Anson Road, #06–04/06, Singapore 079906

Cambridge University Press is part of the University of Cambridge.

It furthers the University's mission by disseminating knowledge in the pursuit of
education, learning, and research at the highest international levels of excellence.

www.cambridge.org
Information on this title: www.cambridge.org/9781108813358
DOI: 10.1017/9781108884440

© D-M Withers 2021

First published 2021

A catalogue record for this publication is available from the British Library.

ISBN 978-1-108-81335-8 Paperback
ISSN 2514-8524 (online)
ISSN 2514-8516 (print)

Virago Reprints and Modern Classics

The Timely Business of Feminist Publishing

Elements in Publishing and Book Culture

DOI: 10.1017/9781108884440

First published online: April 2021

D-M Withers

University of Reading

Author for correspondence: D-M Withers, d.withers@reading.ac.uk

ABSTRACT: Reprinting, republishing and re-covering old books in new clothes is an established publishing practice. How are books that have fallen out of taste and favour resituated by publishers, and recognised by readers, as relevant and timely? This Element outlines three historical textures within British culture of the late 1970s and early 1980s – History, Remembrance and Heritage – that enabled Virago's reprint publishing to become a commercial and cultural success. With detailed archival case studies of the Virago Reprint Library, *Testament of Youth* and the Virago Modern Classics, it elaborates how reprints were profitable for the publisher and moved Virago's books – and the Virago brand name – from the periphery of culture to the centre. Throughout Virago's reprint publishing – and especially with the Modern Classics – the epistemic revelation that women writers were forgotten and could, therefore, be rediscovered, was repeated, again and again, and made culturally productive through the marketplace.

This Element also has a video abstract: www.cambridge.org/withers

KEYWORDS: Virago, reprints, Virago Modern Classics, timeliness, marketing

ISBNs: 9781108813358 (PB), 9781108884440 (OC)

ISSNs: 2514-8524 (online), 2514-8516 (print)

Contents

1 Introduction

To conjure, even for a moment, the wistfulness which is the past is like trying to gather in one's arms the hyacinthine colour of the distance. But if it is once achieved, what sweetness! – like the gentle, fugitive fragrance of spring flowers, dried with bergamot and bay.[1]

I can time-skid, if they cannot, I can go to them, if they cannot come to me.[2]

Reprinting, republishing, re-covering.[3] Selling old texts in new clothes. It is a well-established commercial practice in publishing, as old as the modern industry itself.[4] What conditions enable a book that has slipped out of cultural view to resonate (again) with contemporary readers? How do titles that have fallen *out* of time become activated in another, historical present? In what ways do publishers help audiences reach consensus that a 'forgotten' text can belong to *the* or *this* contemporary moment; that an 'old' book is, in fact, relevant and timely? There is, of course, no single answer to this question, no formula for success that will, in every instance, transform a text's fate from obscurity into cutting edge publishing opportunity.

---

[1] Mary Webb, *Precious Bane* (Virago, 1978/1924), 6.

[2] Stevie Smith, *The Holiday* (Virago, 1979/1949), 41.

[3] I am grateful to Carmen Callil, Virago Press, Alexandra Pringle, Kate Griffin and Peters Fraser & Dunlop for permission to quote from unpublished material in this Element. Thank you to Carmen Callil, Lennie Goodings, Lucy Delap, Zoë Thomas, Rebecca Lidster-Lyons and two anonymous peer reviewers for their generous feedback on this work. Special thanks to Margaretta Jolly, Principal Investigator of the Leverhulme funded Business of Women's Words: Purpose and Profit in Feminist Publishing project (RPG-2017–218), without whom the opportunity to do this research would not exist. Thanks also to the archivists at Special Collections, University of Reading, for helping me access materials during the pandemic, and to Eleanor Dickens and Rachel Foss for supporting my research in the Carmen Callil and Virago archives, held at the British Library.

[4] Richard Altick, *English Common Reader: A Social History of the Mass Reading Public, 1800–1900* (Chicago University Press, 1957).

Reclassification – conferring 'Classic' status upon an already existing text – is one technique through which books from the past are elevated and awarded cultural distinction. This Element is not, however, focused on the practice of canonisation, or that perennial question of the literary critic: 'What is a Classic?'[5] Instead, it is concerned with the practice of timing and how timeliness is culturally constructed within discrete historical contexts. When marketing a book (and indeed any cultural product), timing is everything. Ensuring a book is 'hot' requires planning, creativity, resourcefulness and opportunism; even more so when finances are limited. It involves identifying audiences and synchronising their attention, cultivating nascent and possible desires. Once an audience has become captive, the iron has to continually strike to maintain its heat. This *sense* of timing, realised when the audience adopts the time embedded in the product as their own, acquires a peculiar hue when the book is not germane to the contemporary environment but is, rather, salvaged from a distant, and largely unknown, past. In such circumstances, how can the book be presented as timely? What temporal mechanisms are mobilised to ensure 'then' is commensurate with 'now'? This Element explores these questions by focusing on the reprint publishing of feminist publisher Virago Press, between the years 1973 and 1989.

Virago founder Carmen Callil's early publishing industry experiences were as a 'publicity girl' for London-based publishers André Deutsch, Panther and Granada, 'one of the few jobs available to women who did not want to be secretaries' in the 1960s and early 1970s.[6] When Virago was established, the specialised knowledge about marketing and publicity honed by Callil was emboldened with newly acquired executive power. Started in 1972 by Callil and *Spare Rib* founders Marsha Rowe and Rosie Boycott, Virago incorporated as a limited company in 1973. Between 1973 and 1976, Virago operated as an

---

[5] Frank Kermode, *The Classic: Literary Images of Permanence and Change* (Harvard University Press, 1983). T. S. Eliot (1945). What is a Classic? London: Faber; reprinted in T. S. Eliot (1957). *Of Poetry and Poets*. New York: Farrar, Straus and Cudahy, pp. 53–71.

[6] Carmen Callil, 'The Stories of Our Lives', *The Guardian*, 26 April 2008. www .theguardian.com/books/2008/apr/26/featuresreviews.guardianreview2. Last accessed 28 January 2020.

editorial imprint of Quartet Books and became an independent company in 1976. This independence afforded the key figures who established the Virago enterprise in its early period – Callil, Harriet Spicer and Ursula Owen – the editorial and entrepreneurial freedom to develop their lists.[7]

Many Virago employees were skilled in the penetrative craft of promotion. The company's logo, a bitten apple, mirrored *Spare Rib*'s appropriation of biblical symbols used to justify the demonization and social marginalisation of women for several millennia. As Virago grew from the late 1970s through to the 1980s, the company understood and leveraged the value of 'free publicity'. Reviews, features, radio and TV interviews were all used to great effect to raise the profile of Virago's books and authors beyond what was expected for a 'medium-sized' publisher.[8] In particular, Virago were adept at weaving compelling stories around and about their published books. These tales combined narrative, imagery and design, tastefully presented on attractive posters and postcards. Such marketing materials enabled readers to understand Virago titles and embrace their wider publishing concepts.[9] Importantly, publicity stories constructed the timeliness of Virago's books, cultivating a notion that Virago titles were worthy of the reader's time, attention and, of course, money.

While the Virago Modern Classics (VMC) series, established in 1978 and still core to the company's publishing today, is the most enduring and successful example of Virago's reprint publishing, this Element also draws on other texts Virago reprinted between 1973 and 1989.[10] Overall, it elaborates how and why reprints were a vital ingredient in establishing Virago as a leading mass-market publisher of women's writing. Chapter 2 considers the Virago Reprint Library which republished early twentieth-

---

[7] For more on the histories of Virago, see D-M Withers, 'Enterprising Women: Independence, Finance and Virago Press, c.1976–93', in *Twentieth Century British History* (2019), https://doi.org/10.1093/tcbh/hwz044, and Catherine Riley, *The Virago Story: Assessing the Impact of a Feminist Publishing Phenomenon* (Berghahn, 2018).

[8] 'Virago Press Business Plan 1987', 38. Add MS 89178/1/95, BL.

[9] Mukti Khaire, *Culture and Commerce: The Value of Entrepreneurship in Creative Industries* (Stanford Business Books, 2017), 37.

[10] Up to the end of 2020, 715 titles had been published in the VMC.

century historical research and autobiographies such as Ray Strachey's *The Cause: A Short History of the Women's Movement*, Sylvia Pankhurst's *The Suffragette Movement: An Intimate Account of Persons and Ideals* and *Maternity: Letters from Working Women*, edited by Margaret Llewellyn Davies. Chapter 3 focuses on Virago's republication of Vera Brittain's *Testaments*. Brittain's memoirs proved financially lucrative for the company, bolstered by the popularity of the 1979 BBC serialisation of *Testament of Youth* and accompanying rights sales to mass-market publishers Fontana (Britain) and Seaview (USA). Chapter 4 analyses the material qualities of the VMC, tracing how the books entered and became rooted in public space. This chapter also considers the manner in which the series' design features converged, in contradictory ways, with 'retro-chic' aesthetics strongly associated with other 'heritage brands' such as Laura Ashley.

These different aspects of Virago's reprint publishing between 1973 and 1989 are situated in relation to historical ideas that circulated in Britain in the late 1970s and early 1980s – ideas that were decorative, affective, regulated, mnemonic, tactile, aesthetic, conservative, insurgent and temporal. Within these 'structures of feeling', the idea of women's literary tradition came into focus first for a specific group – women's liberationists – and then broadened out to resonate with wider, popular audiences.[11] The diverse, historically inflected textures of the era acted as cultural holding grounds that enabled Virago's acts of reclassification and recovery to take root in space and time. I designate these distinct ideas as History (Chapter 2), Remembrance (Chapter 3) and Heritage (Chapter 4). Cutting across – and through – these historical terrains meant Virago's reprint publishing could reach audiences and, crucially, break away from the women-centred movement that were the publisher's initial readers (and writers and researchers). Echoing through this Element is Raphael Samuel's invitation to historians to be 'interested in the conditions of existence of history itself', wherein the 'sense of the past, at any given point in time, is quite as much a matter of history as what happened within it'.[12] To understand the cultural

---

[11] Raymond Williams and Michael Orrom, *Preface to Film* (Film Drama, 1954).

[12] Raphael Samuel, *Theatres of Memory: Past and Present in Contemporary Culture* (Verso, 1994), 15.

impact of Virago's reprint publishing of the late 1970s and early 1980s, it is necessary to tease out the different textures of historicity – those distinct 'sense[s] of the past' – that reframed marginalised and largely forgotten books as relevant and timely, stunning readers with awareness that, as Marion Glastonbury wrote in 1979, 'Female emancipation, we *now* realize, is no longer a joke, a fad or a lost cause, but unfinished business of some *urgency*. Rebels of the past, whose ideas until recently seemed as absurdly dated as their hats and hemlines, *speak to our condition*. The forgotten women who laboured in tenements and sweatshops left messages which transmit to us their buried hopes.'[13]

Virago's reprints were successful with readers, as I will elaborate on throughout, because, as feminist texts, their political purpose was legible. Beyond that resonance, the historical inflections of late 1970s and 1980s British society meant republished or 'retro' cultural goods had social meaning. As Samuel observed, the post-war period was characterised by an 'enlargement of the notion of the historical' in everyday life.[14] Anxieties about a diverse range of 'vanishing worlds', be they 'natural' or 'industrial', strengthened a conservationist spirit that had been ignited in the mid-nineteenth century, inspiring a range of social and practical activities that served to revalue and recirculate 'the past'. Virago's reprint publishing – the publisher's organisation and curation of women's literary heritage – took place in a context wherein 'heritage, as it crystallized in the late 1960s' became 'a cultural capital on which all were invited to draw'.[15] Acts of resurrection and preservation, coupled with pride in collection and display, had fomented cultural milieus that would come to embrace the republication of feminist texts, plucked from obscurity and designated by the women-centred publisher as 'Classic'. Virago's reprint publishing was released into a receptive environment, in other words, responsive to the call of the past, and increasingly adept at decoding the cultural value of recirculated goods.

Alongside the profusion of the past in the present, the 1970s was also an era that had 'caught up with' feminist ideas. Feminist movements of

---

[13] Marion Glastonbury, 'When Adam Delved and Eve Span', *Times Education Supplement*, 1136, 28 December 1979. My italics.

[14] Samuel, *Theatres of Memory*, 152–3. [15] Ibid., 237–8.

the nineteenth and early twentieth century, especially those that advocated for women's social, legal and economic independence, had fashioned 'odd women' who were 'ahead of their time' and, therefore, 'untimely'.[16] Feminist knowledge, dispersed and fragmented across history, was 'untimely' in the Nietzschean sense: lives, events and ideas that exceed the historical conditions in which they emerged and, while sometimes receiving recognition in their own time, do not always become a lasting fixture of the cultural, social and political landscape.[17] The 'untimely' history is, however, not wasted or 'used up' when it occurs; it lives on as sedimentary possibility, trapped in the materiality of texts and artefacts (and sometimes passed on as living memory), waiting to be reactivated at a different historical time amenable to its message and meaning. This untimely quality of Virago's republished texts was recognised by Callil, and Virago's readers. Replying to Claire Hardisty in reference to the republication of Brittain's work, Callil wrote: 'you made me realise why we publish some of the books we do, most particularly your thought that Vera Brittain reflected very accurately not only the historical incidents of a very eventful period but the preoccupations of large numbers of people [in the present]'.[18]

In 1970s Britain, ideas about women's liberation vernacularized rapidly. This Element, in part, outlines the unique contribution made by Virago Press as a commercial publisher in this process, retracing the contexts and mediums through which their publishing gave feminist cultural narratives, drawn from the present and the past, wider social mobility. It was an era in which socio-technical conditions (especially the wider availability of birth control) and shifting legal frameworks enabled class- and race-privileged women to experiment with feminist ideas and practices in everyday life. Within this context independent women – much as the Virago directors

---

[16] George Gissing, *The Odd Women* (Penguin, 1993). First published in 1893 and republished by Virago in 1980.

[17] See Victoria Browne, *Feminism, Time and Non-Linear History* (Palgrave, 2014), 66–7; Deborah Withers, *Feminism, Digital Culture and the Politics of Transmission* (Rowman Littlefield International, 2015), 87–121.

[18] 'Carmen Callil to Clare Hardisty, June 1980', Add MS 89904/1/194, BL.

styled themselves as – exercised bodily autonomy with a freedom previous feminist generations dreamt of, but did not directly benefit from.[19] It was in the 1970s, in other words, that a feminist modernity, incubated since the mid-nineteenth century, concretised, for some, as lived possibility. This constituted a historical moment in which the 'untimely' feminism of the past became aligned with feminist times opened up and probed in present, where the 'residues or effects of psycho-symbolic conflict' which reproduced feminist grievances across generations were acted out and woven, deeper, into the fabric of culture, economics, law, politics and society.[20] Society had finally 'caught up' with feminism and the 'untimely' women writers of past eras whose words, imaginations and impulses struck the off-beats and discords of social life.[21]

Feminist times were rarely harmonious within the WLM, however, especially for those unaligned with the movement's diverse political tendencies. For Callil, Virago's founder, the socialist feminism she encountered in her own feminist era felt restrictive, punitive and, from a business point of view, inefficient.[22] Callil's political exile from the feminist present propelled her search for textual solidarity with other, literary outsiders, often housed in the stacks of the London Library, which she gorged on,

[19] For further discussion of socio-technical conditions and autonomy see D-M Withers, 'The Politics of the Workshop: Craft, Autonomy and Women's Liberation', *Feminist Theory* (June 2019), https://doi.org/10.1177%2F1464700119859756; for an exploration of women's liberation and everyday life see Margaretta Jolly, *Sisterhood and After: An Oral History of the Women's Liberation Movement 1968–Present* (Oxford University Press, 2019); for Virago and discourses of independence Withers, 'Enterprising Women'.

[20] Sally Alexander, *Becoming a Woman and Other Essays in 19th and 20th Century Feminist History* (New York University Press, 1995), 245. Alexander viewed the repetition of feminist grievances across history through a psychoanalytic frame.

[21] See Sally Alexander interview by Rachel Cohen (2012), Sisterhood and After: The Women's Liberation Oral History Project, British Library Sound & Moving Image Catalogue, reference C1420/45, transcript page 13/track 4, © The British Library, the University of Sussex; Will May, 'The Untimely Stevie Smith', *Women: A Cultural Review*, 29: 3–4 (2018), 381–97.

[22] Paula Weideger, 'Write On!' *Ms.*, July (1988), 46–51.

night after sleepless night.[23] Like Allen Lane, whose publishing '"genius" lay in the selection of titles [used] to build the brand image, a selection partially based on his own taste,'[24] VMC were very much a 'brand identity' hatched from Callil's obsessive reading, moulded in the image of her cultural and aesthetic predilections. Such tastes were rigorous, too, anchored in a Leavisite conviction about the moral worth of English literature, an orientation shaped, Callil has commented, by her schooling in Australia.[25]

Callil records, with emphatic humour, that she was 'afflicted' by her undergraduate English Literature study in the 'passionately Leavisite English department of Melbourne University'. She claims it motivated her 'to put a bomb under Leavis's agonizingly narrow selection of "great" novelists'. The feminist publishing terrorism unleashed by the VMC was rooted in a 'moral urgency ... articulated through the literary-critical idiom' that shaped Callil's formative reading, and sculpted her social position.[26] Within an individual reader such sensibility is personally significant; for a reader who becomes a publisher they acquire power not only to publish, but extend the parameters of taste beyond their singular, reading experience. In Callil's case, the extension of her reading habitus reached mass markets. This meant the moral valuation of women's writing was distributed to a wide audience, a reconfiguration of reader perceptions into a scene of persistent desire. As Callil developed the VMC in the late 1970s, she was carefully guided by another smart literary-critical hand, the American author Elaine Showalter, who pursued her pioneering study of the

[23] Callil, 'The Stories of Our Lives'.

[24] Alistair McCleery, 'The Return of the Publisher to Book History: The Case of Allen Lane', *Book History*, 5 (2002), 161–85, 168.

[25] Carmen Callil, 'Women, Publishing and Power', in *Writing: A Women's Business*, ed. Judy Simons and Kate Fullbrook (Manchester University Press, 1998), 192.

[26] Carmen Callil, 'Virago Reprints: Redressing the Balance', *Times Literary Supplement*, 12 September 1980; Stefan Collini, *The Nostalgic Imagination: History in English Criticism* (Oxford University Press, 2019), 155.

'Female Tradition' despite not being 'say, F.R. Leavis's sister – the great woman critic who would get everything right'.[27] *A Literature of Their Own: British Women Novelists from Brontë to Lessing*, was published by Virago 27 April 1978 and sold 3034 copies by April 1980; impressive numbers given how the book preceded the explosive growth of feminist academe in the 1980s.[28] Published before *Frost in May*, the first VMC launched in June 1978, *A Literature of Their Own* became the unofficial sourcebook for Virago's literary recovery work.

Virago's embrace of reprint publishing in the mid-1970s was also a matter of financial expediency. As a newly established independent entrepreneurial firm, Virago faced financial challenges. A company statement from 1978 proclaimed:

> We are the only British feminist publishing house for the general market (a second one [The Women's Press] is starting this month). The response to our work has been enormous: we have a wide review coverage on our books ... our only problem is lack of capital to finance all the work we wish to do. We were aware we started as an independent company considerably undercapitalized ... our lack of capital is a constraint in taking on new books, and means limiting the scope of our list until our back list has been built up over a few years. We need capital to support our projects for those intervening years.[29]

---

[27] Elaine Showalter in *A Virago Keepsake to Celebrate Twenty Years of Publishing* (Virago, 1993).

[28] Stefan Collini suggests that by the late 1970s sales of literary critical texts were in decline. He does not account, however, for the growth of feminist criticism and its popularity into the 1980s. See Stefan Collini, '"The Chatto-List": Publishing Literary Criticism in Mid-Twentieth Century Britain', *The Review of English Studies*, 63 (2012), 634–63, 662. Sales for *A Literature of Their Own* taken from 'Dear [blank] from Kate Griffin, 14 May 1980', University of Reading Special Collections MS 5223, Box 11.

[29] 'Company statement', Add MS 89178/1/8, BL.

Establishing a profitable backlist at appropriate speed and scale was, therefore, a financial necessity for Virago. Reprinting old books was a cost- and
time-effective way to do this. The first book published by the independent
Virago in 1977 was, significantly, a reprint of *Life as We Have Known It* by
Co-operative Working Women, edited by Margaret Llewellyn Davies. It
went on to become one of Virago's bestselling titles of the period. Initially
published by the Hogarth Press in 1931 and graced, fortuitously, with an
'introductory letter' by Virginia Woolf, the book spoke to a readership
drawn from the WLM that was stimulated by political fascination with –
and elevation of – working-class women's lives, as I elaborate in Chapter
2.[30] Acquiring publication rights for existing titles was cheaper than invest-
ing in advances for new books written by untried authors. Reprints were
also cheaper to produce due to technological changes in the printing
industry. By the mid-1960s, photocomposition was the dominant method
for typesetting texts, largely because it could be effectively combined with
offset printing.[31] This created novel aesthetic effects for Virago's early
reprints, as page proofs were reproduced from text settings of earlier
hardback editions, as I will analyse in Chapter 4. With the right title,
reprints could prove financially lucrative, as was the case with Virago's
republication of Vera Brittain's memoirs, where rights were sold to mass-
market publishers Fontana, a story covered in Chapter 3.

   Virago were early adopters of 'Midway' or 'B Format', commonly
known today as trade paperbacks. Trade paperbacks were pioneered by
Paladin, a paperback imprint of the Granada Publishing Group launched by

---

[30] See, for example, Sheila Rowbotham, 'The Beginnings of the Women's
   Liberation Movement in Britain', in *Once a Feminist: Stories of a Generation*, ed.
   Michelene Wandor (Virago, 1990), 28–43, on the desire to express solidarity with
   working-class women by WLM activists, and George Stevenson, *The Women's
   Liberation Movement and the Politics of Class in Britain* (Bloomsbury, 2019) for
   detailed exposition of the centrality of class to the WLM.

[31] See Sarah Bromage and Helen Williams, 'Materials, Technologies and the
   Printing Industry', in *The Cambridge History of the Book in Britain: Volume 7, The
   Twentieth Century and Beyond*, ed. Andrew Nash, Claire Squires and I.
   R. Willison (Cambridge University Press, 2019), 47–8.

the late Sonny Mehta in 1970. Callil had worked with Mehta to publicise Paladin books, including *The Female Eunuch* by friend Germaine Greer, which had famously captured the counter-cultural zeitgeist. Paladin were based at 3 Upper James Street, Golden Square, the same building as Panther Books. After work Mehta, Callil and the editorial directors of Panther Books, John Booth and William Miller, would retreat to the pub to hatch new publishing schemes. Booth and Miller went on to establish Quartet in 1972, backed with 'a revolutionary publishing plan: together with the publication of casebound books', Quartet would 'publish simultaneously MIDWAY editions'.[32] Similar in format to the casebound book but with a different binding, 'Midway' formats made 'new books available to the public at a reasonable price, on first publication, when books are reviewed and discussed in the press and television. Midway editions are therefore of enormous benefit to authors and readers.'[33] At the time, Callil explained, they were the 'great, new, chic way of publishing'.[34] 'Midway' editions had financial benefits, too. Virago editor Ursula Owen explained that such books 'were slightly more expensive than A format which were the mass market paperbacks and much cheaper than hardbacks . . . it meant you could do a print run of say, 7–10,000. You didn't have to do 50,000 which you had to do for mass market to make them cheap. So, it was very, very suitable to the kind of books we did.'[35]

In the mid-1970s, a clearly defined mass market for women's writing could hardly be said to exist. Even so, Virago benefitted from the growth of a recognisable readership for left-wing books in that decade, underpinned by the expansion of independent, radical bookshops.[36] Using the

---

[32] 'Statement from Carmen Callil', Add MS 89178/1/2, BL.

[33] 'Statement from Carmen Callil', Add MS 89178/1/2, BL.

[34] Carmen Callil, personal correspondence with author, 7 September 2020.

[35] Ursula Owen interview by Rachel Cohen (2011), Sisterhood and After: The Women's Liberation Oral History Project, British Library Sound & Moving Image Catalogue, reference C1420/36, transcript page 7/track 4, © The British Library, The University of Sussex.

[36] Herbert Hugh, 'A Radical Departure for Virago', *The Guardian*, 23 February 1982.

affordances of trade paperback publishing meant Virago could grow their enterprise within ambitious, yet manageable, parameters. Printing 20,000 copies of a title – a modest run for a mass-market paperback publisher, but a figure at the top limit for Virago – was certainly a financial risk for the company, but it was a careful and calculated one. Virago's publishing of the late 1970s and early 1980s suited the production conditions within the industry of the time; such conditions, in turn, shaped the kinds of books the company produced: smart, visually striking editions that developed an audience for, and recognition of, women's writing as a market category.

The confluence of factors that led to the creation of Virago in general, and its strategic use of reprint publishing to generate financial and cultural capital for the company in particular, was a perfect book publishing storm, situated in a specific historical moment. Even so, many barriers – within the industry and across the wider palette of literary taste – still had to be broken down as Virago charted their move into the cultural imagination. While publishing in trade paperback format in the late 1970s was a pioneering strategy, perhaps 'disruptive' in today's business terms, firms that adopted the format could be placed at a disadvantage in important markets. Most significantly, publishing in trade formats meant exclusion from library sales. Virago still published hardback copies of their books, primarily for reviews but also to secure crucial sales to library suppliers who would only buy in this format.

Such well-trodden book-buying practices were, however, beginning to change, due in part to the dynamism of Virago staff. New Zealander Kate Griffin joined Virago as sales manager in October 1979 and made a significant contribution to Virago's growth prior to their sale to the Chatto, Bodley Head and Jonathan Cape Group in February 1982.[37] Cut from the same indomitable cloth as Callil, Griffin's aptitude for sales management and outgoing, assertive personality helped Virago maximise return on its emerging – and enlarging – backlist. For example, in July 1981 she visited Woolston & Blunts, a library wholesaler based in Nottingham. During her visit she secured agreement to stock VMC; at the time library suppliers were 'obviously aware of the trade

---

[37] See Riley, *The Virago Story*, for a chronological account of Virago's business histories.

paperback [but] unsure how to handle it', which meant many Virago titles were overlooked in the library market.[38] The deal secured by Griffin added £3,000 to Virago's existing turnover from hardback library sales, which then totalled £4,500 a year.[39] Convincing library suppliers to buy trade paperbacks at all was an important achievement that challenged established institutional book-buying practices. It was significant for Virago's overall profitability, too: by end of 1980, reprint publishing (the Virago Reprint Library, VMC and works of Vera Brittain), the majority of which were trade paperbacks, constituted over half the publisher's list.[40]

Virago's reprint publishing was successful, this Element argues, because it ranged across the varied cultural, tactile, affective and symbolic strata in which ideas about history were socially embedded. The scope of timeliness – or the sensibility that Virago's reprints were timely – was therefore extended to a wider cohort of readers. Virago did not only republish forgotten texts that were 'in time' with readers au fait with the politics of women's liberation, or the emergent academic studies of women's history. It also converged with a remembrance culture whose reawakened interest in the First World War was stirred by the sixtieth anniversary of the conflict's end, observed in 1978. The repackaging and re-covering of VMC – those green spines and elegant covers – were also on-trend with a heritage-inflected 'retro-chic' that became popular in the 1980s, and generated much heated cultural and political debate.[41] Virago's publishing was woven into these distinct but also, importantly, *broad* textures of historicity. This meant that a wider range of readers – many who might have initially felt uneasy about reading a 'feminist book' – possessed inclinations and the necessary literacies to decode the meaning of Virago's reprint publishing. In this way, Virago's publishing benefitted from the receptivity to the past that was present in the plural patchwork of historical feelings that existed within British culture of the late 1970s and early 1980s.

---

[38] 'Kate's Nottingham Visit – 21st July 1981', University of Reading Special Collections MS 5223, Box 11.

[39] Ibid.   [40] Ibid.

[41] John Corder and Sylvia Harvey, eds. *Enterprise and Heritage: Crosscurrents of National Culture* (Routledge, 1991); Samuel, *Theatres of Memory*.

Through their publicity and reprint publishing, Virago also contributed significantly to the movement, shape, texture and legibility of different historical times within public space, imbuing culture with discernible, feminised presence. Such cultural force intensified as texts circulated in the commercial marketplace, acquiring special potency when republished Virago books were made into radio shows, television programmes and feature films. Virago's reclamation of 'untimely' women writers synchro-nised, in unexpected ways, with the multivalent historical times that orga-nised sensibilities in late twentieth-century Britain. Their aesthetic choices and publishing rationale conformed to and subverted the conservationist spirit that spread into the fault lines of politics, culture and society, simultaneously at odds with 'Victorian values' while inadvertently normal-ising such cultural logics.[42] This Element explores the varied ways in which Virago's reprint publishing was a timely business: for the publisher, as a financial venture; for the forgotten writer (or her literary executor), who received belated recognition; and, finally, for the reader, who utilised historical frameworks to adopt a text, published in a different time, as belonging to their own.

---

[42] Raphael Samuel, 'Return to Victorian Values', *Proceedings of the British Academy*, 78 (1992), 9–29.

2 History

> Why these circularities; repetitions? Why is there no resolution to feminist grievance?[43]

The Women's Liberation Movement's (WLM) declared a revolutionary 'Year Zero'. History is the first 'sense of the past' that underpinned Virago's reprint publishing in the 1970s. While, in mythic-historic terms, the French Revolution's Year Zero enabled 'ordinary man' to gain a sense of their place within history, the WLM's Year Zero extended the historical process to 'ordinary women'. 'Ordinary women', over-represented from white, middle-class backgrounds, acquired this historical sensibility through the WLM's cultural, political and pedagogical activities. It was a new historical awareness, fashioned from a very specific connection to the past: one in which women had existed, but were forgotten.

The sensibility that a revolutionary feminist modernity belonged, uniquely, to the insurgent late 1960s generation, was underpinned by a perception of historical isolation.[44] Writing in 1982, Anna Coote and Beatrix Campbell suggested that in the early days of the movement activists often felt like they acted in a historical vacuum. This was because previous generations 'lacked the means to transmit their politics to a new generation and so to consolidate their gains'.[45] In the American context, influential radical feminist Shulamith Firestone – whose book *The Dialectic of Sex: The Case for Feminist Revolution* was published in Britain by Jonathan Cape in 1971 – talked evocatively about the 'black-out of feminist history' that kept 'women hysterically circling through

---

[43] Alexander, *Becoming a Woman*, 246.

[44] Especially with regard to the recognition of earlier historical periods, such as suffrage, that were overlooked by some young activists as not being revolutionary at all or not revolutionary enough. See Jolly, *Sisterhood and After*, 245, for a discussion of Rowbotham's early research in the Fawcett Library searching for sources on women's revolutionary movements.

[45] Anna Coote and Beatrix Campbell, *Sweet Freedom* (Blackwell, 1987), 4.

a maze of false solutions'.[46] This sense of dislocation from the past informed the idea that women's liberation was radically new, breaking apart social norms, a 'utopian and romantic disposition' towards the remaking and reclaiming of history.[47]

The historical impulse that shaped the early WLM is often associated with well-known figures such as Sheila Rowbotham, Anna Davin and Sally Alexander. These women, among others, were united through a desire to relate the emergence of women's revolutionary consciousness in the late 1960s to earlier instances of resistance.[48] All three had involvement with History Workshop, the energetic historical research laboratory established by Raphael Samuel at Ruskin College, Oxford, in 1967. History Workshop had an influential role in the development of the burgeoning WLM, and the activist-scholarly practice of feminist history as it grew throughout the 1970s.[49] Most notably, at the fourth workshop, held in November 1969, Rowbotham proposed a meeting to explore women in history, a suggestion notoriously met with derision from male attendees.[50] Undeterred, plans to organise a women's history conference were made, an event that famously became the first National Women's Liberation conference in Britain, held at Ruskin in February 1970.

---

[46] Shulamith Firestone, *The Dialectic of Sex: The Case for Feminist Revolution* (Verso, 2015), 4.

[47] Alexander, *Becoming a Woman*, 225.

[48] Sheila Rowbotham, 'Women's Liberation and the New Politics', in *The Body Politic: Writings from the Women's Liberation Movement in Britain 1969–1972*, ed. Michelene Wandor (Stage 1, 1969/72), 3–30; Sheila Rowbotham, *Women, Resistance and Revolution: A History of Women and Revolution in the Modern World* (Penguin, 1972).

[49] Samuel, while supportive of engagements with women's history, 'never fully metabolised the implications raised by the Movement' in his own work. Sophie Scott-Brown, 'The Art of the Organiser: Raphael Samuel and the Origins of the History Workshop', *History of Education*, 45 (3) (2016), 372–90, 388.

[50] Anna Davin, 'The Only Problem Was Time', *History Workshop Journal*, 50 (2000), 240. For further details see Jolly, *Sisterhood and After*, 26–7, and for personal reflections on the conference see the interviews collected in Wandor, *Once a Feminist*.

History – as an organisational context inspiring action – therefore nourished the roots of women's liberation from its inception.[51] At the 1970 Ruskin conference Rowbotham gave an important speech that gestured towards an epistemic opening that would define the investigative impulse of the WLM, and would shape the purpose of Virago's reprint publishing later in the decade. Called 'The Myth of Inactivity', it claimed that 'Women, like other oppressed groups, figure only incidentally in history. They are amongst the silent people, the people of "no name" who are rarely heard about because they don't [feature] on record.' Due to this, 'much of the listening is still to be done'.[52] Despite basic familiarity with the history of the suffrage campaign and the grand dame of feminism, Mary Wollstonecraft, along with social reformers William Thompson, John Stuart Mill, Marx and Engels, her generation remained 'very ignorant about the ideas and activities of *ordinary women in the past* who rejected the role society gave them'.[53] Rowbotham's talk was, most likely, the first time that such ideas about history were presented to a broader audience, rather than a group whose sense of the past, and of themselves as historical subjects, had been honed within Ruskin's History Workshops.[54] Tellingly, the keynote of the speech focused on France between 1789 and 1871 and, specifically, women who took part in revolutions: 'laundresses, seamstresses, prostitutes, dancing girls, teachers. Many of them suffered personally; others died in exile or on the barricades.'[55] This interest sprung out of respect for their memory,

---

[51] According to Krista Cowman, such an intimate relationship with history has characterised feminism, from medieval writer Christine de Pisan to Virginia Woolf. Krista Cowman, '"Carrying on a Long Tradition": Second-Wave Presentations of First-Wave Feminism in Spare Rib c. 1972–80', *European Journal of Women's Studies*, 17 (3) (2010), 193–210.

[52] Sheila Rowbotham, 'The Myth of Inactivity, Ruskin College 1970', 7ADA/01, The Women's Library.

[53] Rowbotham, 'The Myth of Inactivity'. [54] Alexander, *Becoming a Woman*, 252.

[55] Rowbotham, 'The Myth of Inactivity'. British socialism was one of the many political contexts from which the WLM emerged; since the late nineteenth century, socialism had evolved through a symbolic attachment to French revolutionary traditions, observed through annual events that marked the fall of the 1871 Paris Commune, often with a celebratory tone. See Laura C. Forster,

but it was also an attempt to learn from past revolutionary experiences to guide actions in the present. Such thinking secreted a provocative seed that would germinate within the emergent collective who gathered at the Ruskin conference.

Rowbotham's political and investigative approach to the feminist past – and in particular her fascination with how revolutionary consciousnesses are formed and instigated – were, of course, not shared by all in the movement, or even by those interested in women's history. But it is to Rowbotham that we must attribute an important, revelatory soundbite that gave meaning to an array of political and cultural practices that grew from the movement. These include the activities of the Feminist History Group, which laid the ground for the academic discipline of women's history in Britain; the establishment of the Feminist Archive in 1978, created to ensure that WLM activism was not lost to future generations; and, finally, to the focus of this Element: the reprint publishing of Virago. At some point between 1970 and 1973, 'the Myth of Inactivity' mutated neatly from Rowbotham's quick-flowing pen to become 'Hidden from History'.[56] A punchy statement that rolls off the tongue so quickly, it is very easy to quickly pass over the incision it forced within vernacular understandings of history: namely, that 'ordinary' women were not simply *absent* from the historical record, they were *hidden* from it. And, if they were hidden, they were also waiting to be found. As Rowbotham emphasised to the collective movement from which her thoughts had

'The Paris Commune in the British Socialist Imagination, 1871–1914', *History of European Ideas* (2020), https://doi.org/10.1080/01916599.2020.1746082. See also Rowbotham, *Women, Resistance and Revolution*, 99–134, for later developments of research into women in the Paris Commune.

[56] *Hidden from History* was published by Pluto Press in 1973, a radical left-wing publisher founded 1969, then specialising in 'interventionist pamphlets' and 'accessible revolutionary theory' related to the post-1968 left ferment. Rowbotham knew Pluto founder and International Socialist member Richard Kuper through their mutual involvement in left politics. Richard Kuper, 'A History of Pluto Press: 50 Years of Radical Publishing', www.plutobooks.com/blog/history-pluto-press-fifty-years-radical-publishing/. Last accessed 1 April 2020.

sprung, she was simply 'turning up the top soil in the hope that others will dig deeper'.[57]

2.1 Virago and History

Between 1973 and 1976, Virago's publishing was in a state of research and development. During this time Virago was an editorial imprint of Quartet Books, a company established in 1972 with the aim of exploiting new publishing opportunities afforded by simultaneous publication in hardback and 'Midway' (now termed trade paperback) formats. Virago's initial company statements expressed their interest in 'ideas and research being carried out by women' within the WLM, across the diverse fields of education, history, economics, medicine, sociology, religion, fiction and personal relationships.[58] The earliest meetings of the company, attended by founders Callil, Marsha Rowe and Rosie Boycott, feature long numbered to-do lists, which laid out a broad canvas of publishing ideas. There were plans to establish contact with feminist publishers in Europe – *Éditions des Femmes* in France and *Rivolta Femminile* in Italy – and visit feminist groups in the Netherlands and Switzerland. Left-wing publishers in Britain, such as Pluto and Falling Wall Press, were also approached to discuss potential collaborations. Such attempts to connect with publishers who had similar political sympathies did not lead to meaningful collaborations.

From Virago's personal contacts, however, a publishing programme began to take shape: notes from initial meetings include the publisher's offer for what became Virago's first publication, Mary Chamberlain's *Fenwomen: A Portrait of Women in an English Village*, a title described in Virago's 1975–6 catalogue as exploring women's 'everyday lives' that are 'full of incident, feeling, drama'.[59] Angela Carter's *The Sadeian Woman*, originally planned as Virago's debut publication in August 1975 (in fact published March 1979), fronts the preliminary publishing schedule, as are Carter's suggestions for authors Virago could reach out to. There were plans which

---

[57] Sheila Rowbotham, *Hidden from History: 300 Years of Women's Oppression and the Fight Against It* (Pluto Press, 1973), x.

[58] 'Statement from Carmen Callil', Add MS 89718/1/2, BL.

[59] 'Virago Catalogue, 1975–6', Add MS 89718/6/2, BL.

came to fruition, such as Women in Media's 1977 book *Is This Your Life? Images of Women in the Media*, and ideas that did not materialise, like a book about sex and sexuality, written by their renegade Australian associate, Germaine Greer.[60]

Early meetings burst with energy and different ideas and within them history emerged as a distinct interest. Several new works were proposed. All 'agreed that it's important to do' a book called, simply, 'A History of Women' that would focus on women who were 'notable or some such word' and aimed to stretch back to the seventeenth century, 'if', it was qualified, 'there's enough material'.[61] 'A History of Women' was initially imagined as a co-publication, commissioned by *Spare Rib*, who planned to serialise the book.[62] Other history-focused proposals included a 'Dictionary of Important Women', modelled on Penguin's dictionary series, and a study about the nuclear family and its effect on women. To complement new historical writing, reprinting existing historical works was also suggested. Callil was tasked to enquire at the Fawcett Library about rights for a book called 'Votes for Women', which might have referred to Elizabeth Robins's play, first published in 1909 by Mills & Boon or, perhaps, another suffrage title.[63] The use of the generic suffrage vernacular suggests Callil may have had a sense in the early 1970s that there was a feminist past ready to be reprinted, even if she did not know of specific titles. Later minutes reveal

---

[60] 'Minutes of Virago Meetings, 28 September 1973–8 January 1974', Add MS 89718/1/2, BL.

[61] 'Minutes of Virago Meeting 8 Jan 1974', Add MS 89718/1/2, BL.

[62] The first three issues of *Spare Rib* included a one-page historical feature written by Sheila Rowbotham. Intended as a regular feature, it was soon discontinued, partly due to Rowbotham's busy schedule, but also because Rowe felt readers were more responsive to articles about contemporary issues. See 'Marsha Rowe to Sheila Rowbotham, 17 October 1972', FAS DM 2123/1/55. *Spare Rib* was of course an important site for the development of feminist historiography in the 1970s, especially in relation to suffrage, as Krista Cowman has convincingly argued. Cowman, 'Carrying on a Long Tradition'.

[63] It seems unlikely that Virago would have published a playscript at this time; while the scope of their publishing in this period was broad, its focus was fiction and non-fiction.

Callil had made an application to join the Fawcett Library and, along with Andrea Adam, was to visit to discuss possibilities for reprinting titles held in their collections.[64]

Virago's first catalogue announced the publication of ten eclectic – and original – non-fiction titles. Half could be said to have historical themes even if they were, in no sense, straightforward *histories*. *Fenwomen*, as discussed, foregrounded the historical importance of 'ordinary' women's lives. *Forgetting's No Excuse*, the autobiography of *Guardian* women's page editor Mary Stott, invoked the political imperative to remember that the WLM mobilised. *Fathers and Daughters: Russian Women in Revolution* by Cathy Porter explored the iconicity of female revolutionaries, while Merlin Stone's *The Paradise Papers: The Suppression of Women's Rites*, tapped into deeper, historical fault lines: the archaeological interest in matriarchal societies pioneered in Britain by artist and activist Monica Sjöö and feminist theologian, Asphodel Long. Carter's *The Sadeian Woman* was the final, historically situated book featured in the catalogue, even if it was not published until later in the decade. The other books Virago published were practical offerings. *The British Woman's Directory* (in fact published as *The Women's Directory*) was an A–Z of women's liberation for the uninitiated. It included advice about legal changes, health, childcare and work, among many other areas – the kind of information available in the many Women's Centres established by WLM activists in British towns and cities since the early 1970s. Significantly, the book is introduced by a four-page timeline of women's history; Year Zero is 1792, marked by the publication of Mary Wollstonecraft's *A Vindication of the Rights of Women*. *The Gender Trap*, a book aimed at the teenage market, intended to raise awareness of the negative – and lifelong – impact of gender stereotypes. *Is This Your Life?* had similar pedagogical intentions but spoke to adult women, enabling this social group to become aware of internalised sexism and its enforcement through media images. The outlier was *My Secret Garden*, a bestselling book by US author Nancy Friday about women's sexual fantasies, introduced for British audiences by journalist Jill Tweedie.

---

[64] 'Minutes of Virago Meeting 8 Jan 1974'.

Figure 1 Virago's 1975–6 book catalogue, Add MS 89178/6/2, British Library © Virago.

2.2 *Virago*

The wide scope of Virago's first ten books is striking. While certainly Virago published new research about women's lives, in line with their declared intentions, the topics are otherwise fairly diffuse. This was publishing for a clearly defined readership, a target audience of readers connected to, or whose interest had been piqued by, the politics of women's liberation. Directories, handbooks, manuals – writing modes that evolved from the movement's 'workshops' that aimed to empower and reskill women – feature prominently.[65] The other thing to note is that original commissions dominated the list. Creating a new list is, at the best of times, difficult publishing work. Even more so for Virago, who began their publishing journey in the forbidding economic environment of the early 1970s. Between 1974 and 1975, against a backdrop of inflation affecting the wider economy, the price of book production rose sharply. Paper, binding, printing, distribution and warehousing costs increased to around 30–50 per cent. Postal charges spiralled, which meant it became more expensive to post a book than produce one. This amounted, some in publishing at the time claimed, to 'industrial genocide'. Even when book prices increased in response to changed market conditions, the squeezed consumer was faced with difficult decisions. The year 1975 brought a particular challenge: for the first time the average new novel, priced at £3.95, cost more than the latest LP.[66]

Virago were certainly not immune from the financial troubles afflicting the wider industry. Their position within Quartet shielded the company from some fiscal burdens. Even so, their main aim was to generate enough profit to become independent. To do this, Virago had to build up their list as quickly and efficiently possible. As already suggested, Virago's period as an editorial imprint of Quartet was characterised by frantic learning and development, especially in terms of understanding how the publishing business functioned. In the many notes from meetings with publishing colleagues produced at this time, one piece of advice, offered by an employee of Michael Joseph, likely in 1976, stands out: that 'sheer profit'

---

[65] Withers, 'The Politics of the Workshop'.

[66] J.A. Sutherland, *Fiction and the Fiction Industry* (The Athlone Press, 1978), 26–7.

was far greater with reprints, with the initial investment estimated at
5 per cent of overhead costs compared with 35 per cent of overhead costs
for new books.[67] Reprints were, as already established, one of the many
ideas courted by Virago in its earliest meetings. It is not until Virago
became an independent company in 1976, however, that reprints became
core to their publishing. Even at this time reprint publishing was considered
a sub-section of the emergent women's studies market. The list below,
probably written between 1976 and 1977, that outlines Virago's rationale for
acquiring new titles, suggests as much:

> American and European sales potential
> British market potential – publicity PLUS what gap in market
> Serialisation possibilities – (ie *[sic]* SPLITTING UP taken on
>   because we wanted to get stuff in popular women's mags)
> Health and Handbook market
> Women's Studies market INCLUDING feminist classics
> Backlist potential.[68]

Even the 1977 catalogue includes a diverse range of areas and indicates
Virago had not yet settled on a workable (and winning) publishing formula.
While 'our plans for the future include more emphasis on practical hand-
books, pamphlets, folders, illustrated books, translations and reprints', the
catalogue states, it is the 'reprint series of out-of-print classics' that tops the
list of new series launched in 1977. The leading title was *Life as We Have
Known It* by Co-operative Working Women, published by the Hogarth
Press in 1931, Virago's first as an independent company.

   Virago's turn to reprints did not evolve from financial revelations alone.
Ursula Owen came to work as an editor part-time at Virago in 1974,
becoming full-time in 1976, and had knowledge of reprints. Owen cut her

---

[67] 'Money Problems', Add MS 89718/1/4, BL.
[68] 'Factors We Consider When Taking on Books', UOR MS5223/10/11-1. While
undated, these statements are appended to a wish-list of fiction and non-fiction
titles which includes Brittain's *Testament of Experience*, published in 1978, hence
locating it in 1976–7.

publishing cloth with a part-time job at Frank Cass, a small, idiosyncratic family firm then specialising in reprint publishing targeted at international, academic markets, in the early 1970s. Frank Cass had been at the centre of the 'reprint revolution' that began in the late 1950s. Involved in the book trade since nineteen, Cass's first job was in the LSE's Economist bookshop. There he met international scholars hungry for out-of-print, hard-to-find academic books, stung by the depletion of London's book stocks, destroyed during Second World War air raids.[69] Discovering an aptitude for sourcing hard-to-find books, he set up a second-hand bookshop to target the reading needs of this clearly defined academic market. He subsequently entered publishing, reprinting out of print and copyright books, with particular emphasis on history and the social sciences. Through his network of academic contacts, Cass acquired a clandestine knowledge of the market demand for obscure scholarly texts. When Cass approached existing copyright holders, they were often unaware of a potential market and readily granted permission to reprint.[70] A similar circuit of events was repeated by Owen and Virago twenty years later. This time the clearly defined market was not frustrated international scholars from the LSE; rather, it was the academically inclined women who composed Virago's advisory group whose specialist knowledge, in return, shaped Virago's list.

Owen is often framed in the Virago story as the figure who brought feminist contacts and political integrity in-house. As someone who attended consciousness-raising meetings at Rowbotham's home in Arsenal in the early 1970s, such characterisations ring true. Owen's experience at Frank Cass, however, gave her a very particular kind of publishing industry education that proved vital to the development of Virago's reprint publishing. Working at Frank Cass exposed Owen to the varied practices of reprint publishing, direct from a pioneer company in the sector. She learnt how to research potential titles and spent 'many happy hours reading for possible reprints across the road [from the publisher's office] in the reading room of

---

[69] Colin Holmes, 'Obituary: Frank Cass', *Immigrants & Minorities*, 27 (1) (2009), 118–22, 119.

[70] Gerry Black, *Frank's Way: Frank Cass and Fifty Years of Publishing* (Vallentine Mitchell, 2008), 37–9.

the British Museum'.[71] Owen 'absorb[ed]' the wider processes involved in reprinting works (or had such advice on hand if needed), including how to acquire rights and select appropriate introducers to explain the merits of unfamiliar works.[72] She likely possessed the technical know-how of how reprints were produced from photo-setting technologies that had, by the mid-1970s, been widely adopted in the publishing industry. When Owen joined Virago, she brought to the project a unique blend of social capital that traversed activist and publishing communities, vital to the expansion of the publisher in the 1970s and beyond. Callil's interest in reprinting books from the Fawcett Library, noted in early meetings, gained cohesion, focus and practical support with Owen's knowledge.

2.3 Virago Reprint Library

Virago's advisory group had expertise in many areas, including history. Sally Alexander, part of the Advisory Group for nearly two decades, remembers that 'it was about talking, bringing books to their attention'.[73] *Life as We Have Known It* fronted what became formalised, in the 1977–8 catalogue, as the 'Virago Reprint Library', the publisher's first clearly defined – and numbered, thus collectable – reprint series. *Life as We Have Known It* had been reprinted by US publishers W. W. Norton & Company in 1975. Edwin Barber worked for W. W. Norton & Company and was an old friend of Callil. He informed her that Hogarth Press, a subsidiary of Chatto & Windus since 1946, were rights holders for the publication. On receipt of this information, Callil wrote to Jane Gregory, who worked in the Subsidiary Rights department at Chatto & Windus, to express Virago's interest in the title.[74] At this time Virago were in the process of acquiring finance to become an independent company. Writing to Norah Smallwood, who she would

---

71 Ursula Owen, *Single Journey Only: A Memoir* (Salt, 2019), 253.

72 Owen, *Single Journey*, 259.

73 Alexander interviewed by Cohen, 103–4, track 4.

74 Following Callil's approach, *Life as We Have Known It* was briefly considered for CBC's Triad paperback imprint; before accepting Virago's offer Gregory wrote to Stephanie Dowrick, then working for Triad, to see if there was interest. Dowrick went on to co-found Virago's main commercial competitor The

eventually replace as Managing Director of Chatto & Windus in 1982, Callil informed the veteran publisher that Virago had secured finance to become an independent company. 'Our very first action', Callil enthused, 'has been to offer for *Life as We Have Known It* and *Three Guineas*, we've been devoted to these books for some time'.[75]

Life as We Have Known It features testimonies from working-class women involved in the Women's Co-operative Guild. The stories had dual resonance with the historical interests of 1970s women's liberation activists. Firstly, the book is a rare historical foregrounding of 'ordinary' working women's experience. Secondly, through Virginia Woolf's 'introductory letter', the middle-class structure of the WLM which strongly influenced how the historical subject of women's liberation was constructed, came into contact with an earlier time when anxieties about political location, class and solidarity are recorded as a feminist concern. Woolf's account of attending a meeting of the Women's Co-operative Guild in Newcastle in 1913 is often cited as evidence of her social snobbery and political ambivalence; critics point to her perverse fascination with the 'thick-set and muscular' bodies of working women, whose 'hands were large' and 'had the slow emphatic gestures of people who are often stiff and fall in a tired heap on hard-backed chairs'.[76] Yet, as Alice Wood eloquently argues, Woolf's use of the letter as a 'flexible epistolary form' is a discursive tactic that aims to both engage and disarm the imagined middle-class readership, supporting them to 'admit and probe the discomfort that they may feel when encountering the frank recollections of poverty and hardship' recounted in the book.[77]

Women's Press in 1977. See 'Jane Gregory to Stephanie Dowrick 12 May 1976', UOR, CW/317/6.

[75] 'Correspondence Between Norah Smallwood to Carmen Callil 6–9 September 1976', UOR, CW/317/6. Eventually, Penguin made Smallwood an offer she was unable to refuse for paperback rights to publish *Three Guineas*.

[76] Virginia Woolf, 'Introductory Letter to Margaret Llewellyn Davies', in *Life as We Have Known It*, ed. Margaret Llewellyn Davies (Virago, 2012), xvi–xvii.

[77] Alice Wood, 'Facing Life as We Have Known it: Virginia Woolf and the Women's Co-operative Guild', *Literature & History*, 23 (2) (2014), 18–34, 26–7.

For women's liberation activists, working-class women were similar emblems of political authenticity and alterity. Through the Night Cleaners' Campaign especially, middle-class anxieties about the (im)possibility of effective solidarity across class boundaries was very much present in the voluminous activist commentaries produced about the struggle. The Night Cleaners' Campaign seemed to offer the WLM a political education about the exploitation of working-class, often immigrant women, in the labour market. It also created a context through which activists reflected on the movement's strategic effectiveness vis-à-vis cross-class coalitions. 'A whole cluster of questions arise from the contradiction,' wrote Alexander in 1974, 'between our aspiration to be a movement which involves all oppressed women and our present predominantly middle class membership. For example, how do we extend our practice beyond its existing constricted boundaries?'[78] Alexander's write-up of the campaign strikes an earnest and worried tone; it lacks the artful dodging of Woolf's letter which, aesthetically, has more in common with the Berwick Street Film Collective's 1975 film *Nightcleaners*, a work of political cinema inspired by the Night Cleaners' long – and ultimately unsuccessful – strike. The Night Cleaners' Campaign became a vector through which middle-class feminist anxieties about privilege and speaking for others resurfaced and circulated as a historical structure of feeling. In the cultural, historical and affective space opened by the strike, the republication of *Life as We Have Known It* garnered meaning – as a signal of attempted, unresolved and frustrated solidarities, and of the driving hope that marginalised historical subjects may speak in their own voices, according to their own experience, and be heard.

Life as We Have Known It was welcomed by feminist critics. Jane Caplan, writing in *Spare Rib*, praised the 'quietly remarkable book' with its 'calm and unembellished prose'.[79] Virago were 'to be congratulated for reprinting this' Caplan enthused, outlining her eager anticipation of Virago's publication in June 1978 of another Women's Co-operative

---

[78] Sally Alexander, 'The Nightcleaners' Campaign', in *Conditions of Illusion: Papers from the Women's Movement* (Feminist Books, 1974), 309.

[79] Jane Caplan, 'Life as We Have Known It', *Spare Rib*, 63 (1977), 42.

Guild title, *Maternity: Letters from Working Women*, first published in 1915.[80] *Life as We Have Known It* became a bestseller for Virago, selling 7,033 copies by April 1980 and 10,356 by March 1982. Other titles in the Reprint Library about working-class women's experience had similar sales success: by 1980, *Maternity* had sold a solid 4,554 copies. The bestselling title of this kind was *Round About a Pound a Week* by Maud Pember Reeves, first published in 1913, an example of early twentieth-century feminist social science.[81] Published in January 1979 with a new introduction by Alexander, it had sold 13,462 copies by March 1982.

An interesting point of comparison is the sales figures of reprints about the Suffrage Movement, written by its key activists. By 1980, Emmeline Pankhurst's autobiography *My Own Story*, published in January 1979, had sold 2,620 copies, with less than 200 copies claimed in the first four months of 1980. Other cuts of suffrage's ideological cloth commanded similar sales figures. Sylvia Pankhurst's *The Suffragette Movement: An Intimate Account of Persons and Ideals*, published in November 1977 had sold 2,621 paperback and 405 hardback copies. Ray Strachey's *The Cause: A Short History of the Women's Movement*, published in February 1978, sold 2,390 in paperback.[82] Perhaps the relatively low sales of the suffrage volumes can be explained pragmatically: weighing in at 432 pages, Strachey's 'short' history did not live up to its name. At 648 pages, Sylvia Pankhurst's historical account may have been intimate, but it was also sprawling. *Life as We Have Known It*, *Maternity* and *Round About a Pound*, in contrast, were concise volumes, all ranging between 184 and 232 pages. The writing in these books, as already

---

[80] Caplan, 'Life as We Have Known It'.

[81] See Ann Oakley, *Women: Peace and Welfare: A Suppressed History of Social Reform, 1880–1920* (Policy Press, 2018).

[82] A brief note on sales figures: while even today the publishing industry is characterised by partial, non-standardized data collection across different areas, including sales, between 1976 and 1982 Virago kept a tight, monthly assessment of figures that were regularly discussed at sales meetings. The company was shocked about the quarterly reporting they received when they became part of CBC. See 'Virago Press Business Plan 1987' for criticisms of CBC's data provision. On book statistics see Miha Kovač, Angus Phillips, Adriaan van der Weel, and Rüdiger Wischenbart. 'Book Statistics', *Logos*, 28 (4) (2017), 7–17.

noted, was praised for its accessibility, couched, as it was, in the idiom of personal experience that lay at the heart of women's liberation's 'ordinary' politics. New history books about the suffrage movement, such as Jill Liddington and Jill Norris's *One Hand Tied Behind Us: The Rise of the Suffrage Movement* from June 1978, fared slightly better, with 2,602 copies sold by April 1980. While it is difficult to draw strong generalisations about the popularity of different periods of feminist history from these figures, the similar sales level across new and old suffrage titles offers a strong barometer of reader interest. What emerges from the comparison is that between 1977 and 1980, the sales of suffrage-related titles are consistent with each other, but sales of books by and about working women from the early twentieth century are significantly greater.[83]

By the late 1970s, ideas about history incubated in the WLM had bubbled up and spread out, touching institutions across society. Through Virago's 'Reprint Library', the publisher was able to grasp new audiences, especially in the educational sphere. Indeed, as Virago made decisions about which books to reprint, they consulted teachers to ascertain a text's value for schools and the 'Liberal Studies' market.[84] Evidence of such reach is discernible in the correspondence of the London-based Feminist History Group (FHG), established in 1973 and composed of WLM activists committed to the political pursuit of women's history. The FHG, in similar vein to the History Workshop, aimed to create a generous laboratory for sharing resources and research ideas, supporting nascent feminist historians whose work lacked institutional backing or location. Being based at the Women's Research and Resources

---

[83] 'Dear [blank] from Kate Griffin, 14 May 1980', UOR MS 5223, Box 11; 'Sales figures, March 1982, for Virago Press Front and Back List Titles', Add MS 89178/1/45, BL. These sales figures could also be compared to sales of new and licensed fiction published in 1977/8: for example, by January 1981 *The New Woman's Health Handbook* had sold 8,607 copies; *Make It Happy: What Sex Is All About* by Jane Cousins 11,922; Kate Millet's *Sexual Politics* 11,493 and *Sita* 11,700. 'Sales figures for 1977 and 1978 Titles, Captured Jan 1981', UOR, MS 5223, Box 11.

[84] 'Carmen Callil to Jane Gregory 13 September 1976', UOR, CW/317/6.

Centre, an information hub that opened in 1975 and supported the development of women's studies in Britain, enabled the FHG to publicise their meetings, use and contribute to collective research facilities and receive correspondence.[85] In the summer of 1978, a spate of schoolgirls across England wrote to the FHG. 'Judging from enquiries to the WRRC,' Davin wrote, 'there are now a number of schools where explicitly women's studies courses are organized.'[86] The young women asked for book recommendations about suffrage and the women's movement, their interest in feminist history conscientiously ushered by schoolmistresses who set study projects for their O levels.

Teachers wrote to the FHG too, asking for advice on books that could inspire their students. After reading about the FHG in *Spare Rib*, Mrs J. Bowden of John Ruskin High School, Croydon, convenor of a voluntary lower sixth form history class on 'Women in Society Since 1850', wrote to the group on 4 October 1978. In response, Davin penned a substantial, three-page letter, outlining the range of material available. Top of her recommendation list for this cohort was *Life as We Have Known It* and *Maternity*. Davin – who of course introduced Virago's edition of *Life as We Have Known It* – enthused about the book's 'exceptionally vivid and good reading, as well as extraordinary in that you rarely find working women's own account of their lives'. Further, she added quickly, Virago had reprinted the titles in paperback, 'both under £2' – a company policy to ensure Virago books were financially accessible to readers.[87] While other history books, such as *One Hand Tied Behind Us* were, for this age group, 'a bit heavy going,' and further sources were not at that time published, or were expensive or hard to find, *Life as We Have Known It* and *Maternity* were recommended not only as suitable books, but *usable* books.

Virago's 'Reprint Library' both caught and contributed to the widening interest in women's history. It 'really did a great service', reflected Alexander, 'they were a landmark series of books in putting into the public realm again,

[85] Anna Davin, 'The London Feminist History Group', *History Workshop Journal*, 9 (1) (1980), 192–4.

[86] 'Anna Davin to Sue Jessop, 17 March 1979', 7ADA/01, The Women's Library.

[87] 'Anna Davin to Mrs. Bowden', 7ADA/01, The Women's Library.

you know, feminist ideas . . . – and research – that had been forgotten.'[88]
Beyond stimulating the interest of school-age children, Virago's republication
of existing feminist research gave the company an 'academic edge'. It signalled
to the wider industry that there was a 'massive need [and] appetite for books
which hadn't really been there' before explained Phillipa Brewster, founder of
non-fiction imprint Pandora Books, who targeted the emergent academic
women's studies market in the 1980s.[89] Within Virago itself, the Reprint
Library was the basis of a far wider adventure in reprint publishing that
was rapidly coming into focus. The introductory text to Virago's
June 1978–June 1979 catalogue declares, confidently, that 'four new titles
have been added to our Reprint Library and, *notably*, we announce Virago
Modern Classics, a new series of *outstanding* out of print twentieth century
novels'.[90] Before the VMC were launched, the Virago Reprint Library was
a catch-all for out-of-print classics – history, memoir and fiction. Ten new
titles are listed for the Virago Reprint Library on the final page of Virago's
1978–9 catalogue. Out of these Olive Schreiner's *Dreams* (number 9) was
never published; Sarah Grand's *The Beth Book* (number 10) came out
April 1980 but was reframed as a VMC.[91] The Virago Reprint Library
never totalled more than eight titles. From June 1978 Virago's reprint publishing turned in earnest to the VMC. Callil described her visionary revelation
after she read Antonia White's *Frost in May* that propelled her to publishing
action: 'and that weekend I thought, I'm going to start a fiction list.'[92] This
quick decision, that seems now to be almost inevitable, nonetheless marked

88 Alexander interviewed by Cohen, 103–4, track 4.
89 Philippa Brewster interview by Margaretta Jolly (2019), The Business of
    Women's Words: Purpose and Profit in Feminist Publishing, British Library
    Sound & Moving Image Catalogue, reference C1834/10, © The British Library.
90 'Virago: New Books & Complete List, June 1978–June 1979', Add MS 89178/6/
    4, BL. My emphasis.
91 The publication of *The Beth Book* was delayed because Callil had invited
    Showalter to write the introduction, and she could only deliver at a later date. See
    'Carmen Callil to Elaine Showalter, 15 June 1979', The Women's Library,
    7ESG/A/02/Showalter.
92 Carmen Callil in *The British Book Trade: An Oral History*, ed. Sue Bradley (BL
    Publishing, 2008), 213.

a significant change in the trajectory of Virago's reprint publishing which, up to that point, had focused more on non-fiction books. In their January 1982–March 1983 catalogue, Virago announced a new Classics series: Virago Non-Fiction Classics. These were 'diaries and journals, most particularly of women travellers, biographies and autobiographies, prose and poetry, journalism, essays and *belles lettres* – those delightful writings which defy exact categorisation but which . . . promise a multitude of literary pleasures'.[93]

VMC opened the door for Virago to reach mainstream audiences, as will be discussed in more detail in Chapter 4. With VMC, Virago broke away from the WLM's concepts of history; these ideas were no longer the central point through which the company's reprint publishing was refracted. In truth, history in the WLM was a tensile, multivocal phenomenon, sensitive to the action of recovery *and* the invention of tradition.[94] The Year Zero sensibility, invoked at the start of the chapter, attuned social movement actors to an acute sense of their own history-making. History was not just about the past, but about writing – especially – the ordinary experience of the present. 'In writing for other women', argued Gail Chester and Sigrid Nielsen in the introduction to the important collection *In Other Words: Writing as a Feminist*, 'we reinterpret our own experience in a way which brings us closer together. And women's experience is not only the sum total of each woman's memories, but a collective possession, a tradition which shapes the way we view our individual lives. We are all engaged in creating this tradition.'[95] This temporal sense of history – that history was of the *now*

---

[93] 'Virago Press: New Books & Complete List, January 1982–March 1983', 6, Add MS 89178/6/8, BL.

[94] June Purvis argued that the socialist historians connected to the History Workshop, who are the main focus of this chapter, shaped the ideological basis of feminist historiography as it evolved as an academic discipline in the late 1970s and early 1980s, with particular implications for the writing of militant suffrage histories: see June Purvis, 'Gendering the Historiography of the Suffragette Movement in Edwardian Britain: Some Reflections', *Women's History Review*, 22 (4) (2013), 576–90.

[95] Gail Chester and Sigrid Nielsen, 'Introduction: Writing as a Feminist', in *In Other Words: Writing as a Feminist*, ed. Gail Chester and Sigrid Nielsen (Hutchinson, 1987), 17–18.

and that new, invented traditions were to be collectively *possessed* – could, sometimes, turn a critical eye on Virago's reprint publishing.

By 1981, the VMC had become part of the cultural landscape. Commercial success led to greater political scrutiny, especially by some WLM activists. *Rolling Our Own: Women as Printers, Publishers and Distributors* (*ROO*), a significant, collectively authored overview of feminist publishing written in 1981, outlined the crucial, dialogical role of feminist publishers in advancing the movement's cultural politics: 'women have and are producing much literary, theoretical and visual work, and it is the job of the women's press to give them the network of communication they need.'[96] *ROO* acknowledged that 'Virago *have* been criticised for this concentration on reprints at the expense of newer work; however the importance given to reprints is partly a reflection of their aim to establish the existence of women's culture more firmly in the public mind, and partly a financial consideration, since not only do reprints usually cost less than publishing a book for the first time, they also sell fairly well.'[97] Here the *ROO* authors pragmatically acknowledge the reprint's financial expediency. Nevertheless, the sense that Virago failed to support new writers from within the WLM – that the past was being recovered at the expense of nurturing the present – returns: 'at the outset, they did intend to give *much more* support to new women writers.'[98]

The political value of Virago's publishing is framed here within the WLM's Janus-faced conception of history: a determination to disseminate what felt and seemed radically new, while grounding such experience in what was revealed – most successfully (and ironically) through Virago's reprint publishing – as a series of historically continuous, feminist grievances. Internally, Virago were conscious of the tug between new and old in their publishing. In the early 1980s, Callil was keen to convey clearly to critics that the VMC was 'not a mausoleum: it's a presentation of a tradition and live

---

[96] Eileen Cadman, Gail Chester and Agnes Pivot, *Rolling Our Own: Women as Printers, Publishers and Distributors* (Minority Press Group, 1981), 28–9. See also Simone Murray, *Mixed Media: Feminist Presses and Publishing Politics* (Pluto, 2004), 69–82, for an assessment of the Women's Press vis-à-vis its financial politics.

[97] *Rolling Our Own*, 31. [98] *Rolling Our Own*, 31. Italics mine.

authors will continue to have a place in it'.[99] In a memo intended for all Virago Press staff members sent in April 1983, Callil even quantified the 'dead or alive' ratio of authors Virago published. Of the 249 books in print by end of 1983, she wrote, in the VMC 'there are 85 dead authors and 46 live authors (though this includes Rebecca West and Christina Stead, and should therefore be 87/44!). From the rest of our list we have 37 dead authors and 81 live authors. This means that of our 249 books in print by the end of 1983, 124 are dead, 125 alive!'[100]

Virago, perhaps more than any other publisher, fulfilled the 'first wish of feminist history – to fill the gaps and silences of written history, to uncover new meanings for femininity and women, to propel sexuality to the forefront of the political mind'.[101] Their mode of fulfilment was to organise, repackage and remember – put together in a new form – what was already there, thus leveraging the cultural, economic and social power of women's writing from the past, in service of the present and the future. As Virago instigated a 'brisk trade . . . in what was hitherto hidden from history', their reprint publishing never moved far away from the focus of this original wish.[102] In the realm of the marketplace forgetting is acute. Every new cultural product is a singularity that has to be promoted energetically to ensure consumers recognise its timeliness and claim the time of the product as their own. This was fertile ground upon which to continually enact the discovering of feminism's hidden past and repeat its *epistemic* revelation.[103] The historical recurrence of 'feminist discontent' was a feeling and call to action grasped from the knowledge-makers of the WLM. Such activating insight, when locked into market forces, reverberated beyond the social movement, becoming a seductive, iterative and enduring publishing concept, capable of reopening forgotten times, again

[99] 'Memo from Carmen Callil to Ursula Owen, Lennie Goodings, Kate Griffin and Harriet Spicer, Regarding the Image of Virago Press', Add MS 89178/1/71, BL.
[100] 'Memo from Carmen Callil to Virago Press Staff Members, 13 April 1983', Add MS 89178/1/47, BL.
[101] Alexander, *Becoming a Woman*, 225.
[102] Glastonbury, 'When Adam Delved and Eve Span'.
[103] Khaire, *Culture and Commerce*, 44.

and again. It was a concept hewn from restless history workshops and activist desires, but whose meaning could be productively generalised, especially when notions of recovery, retrieval, inheritance and remembrance mingled with other senses of the past composing British society in the late 1970s, and through the 1980s: Remembrance, the focus of the next chapter, and Heritage, in Chapter 4. Virago became a mass-market commercial success because they found ways to extend their market reach beyond the 30,000 people that, according to Jolly, had connections with the WLM by 1981.[104] While these numbers represented a defined and targetable market, not all of these people would of course have bought Virago books. The next two chapters tell the story of how Virago infiltrated wider social feelings organised through historical time, ideas and aesthetics. In doing so they widened the timely scope of the untimely woman writer.

---

[104] See Jolly, *Sisterhood and After*, 96, for further discussion on how this estimate was reached.

3 Remembrance

Why are we so haunted?[105]

Of all the 'senses of the past' that course through British culture, remembrance has been a fixture for over a century. The annual Remembrance Sunday event resets social, historical and personal time in line with the end of the First World War. Every second Sunday in November, the remembrance ritual takes place and claims time, a calendric mechanism that organises feelings about war, militarism, heroism and sacrifice, inserting such values as regularised social rhythms. Remembrance Sunday is a clear instance in British democratic national life that is subject to state-sanctioned synchronisation; when time is deliberately put aside in the calendar to be shared, in solemnity and reflection. For that reason, it is probably the broadest and most populist texture of historicity that Virago's reprint publishing converged with; a temporal pulse drenched with intentional affect, recognisable to anyone who grows up and lives in Britain, a global commemorative culture with local, regional and national resonances.[106]

Effective publishing, marketing and publicity similarly court intimate affinity with the calendar, mobilised with intention to organise audience attention around a text's value and relevance. Such practices tug at social temporalities, targeting potential readers who might 'adopt' the cultural object presented to them as their own. In turn, social memories of significant historical events create discourse and public feelings that become widely available.[107] Virago benefitted from and utilised this distributed social knowledge with great effect to position their books to readers. In June 1980, for example, the Virago staff planned a publicity push for a new title, the social history cookbook hybrid *Bombers and Mash: The Domestic Front 1939–45*, written by Raynes Minns. The notes from the publicity meeting urgently call upon

---

[105] Shirley Williams, 'Preface', *Testament of Youth* (Virago, 1978), 9.

[106] Jay Winter, 'Commemorating Catastrophe: 100 Years On', *War & Society*, 36 (4) (2017), 239–55.

[107] James Fentress and Chris Wickham, *Social Memory* (Blackwell, 1992).

Kate, Lennie and Ursula to find out what was happening round the country on 13 Nov 1940. Publicity geared to what was happening in YOUR city 40 years ago today – find all possible regional anniversaries. This [is] useful for both local newspapers and local bookshops who can use the info to get people interested. The Blitz was on for instance. Sept–Nov 1940 London bombed every night. Ursula to give Kate list of worst struck towns. Kate to get book displays in those towns – e.g., Plymouth, Coventry etc.[108]

Marketing *Bombers and Mash* is conceived here as a targeted, calendric activity, imagined as a process through which the interest of a potential reader becomes aligned with significant events in the national and local past.[109] The direct address of the marketing campaign – *what was happening in YOUR city* – personalises what may be, in different historical contexts, impersonal events, and constructs identification and meaning. The marketing of *Bombers and Mash* touches upon an aspect of remembrance culture in Britain: the resourceful energy, good feeling and community spiritedness of the Second World War. The social memory of the First World War, in contrast, has generally been couched in more tragic registers. Even so, this aspect of remembrance culture is subject to its own variations across time. The heroic mode of remembrance that characterised the immediate aftermath of the First World War, for example, began to shift towards disenchantment at the end of the 1920s, in part due to the outpouring of writing associated with the 'War Books Boom'.[110] Within a context where it became culturally permissible to articulate disillusionment about the war, Vera Brittain sketched a chapter outline for *Testament of Youth*, a book first published by left-leaning publishers Victor Gollancz in 1933. Brittain's biographer Mark Bostridge has suggested that the 'War Books Boom' did not only express feelings about the 'needless waste' and 'hopeless sacrifice'

[108] 'Promotions Meeting 19.6.80', Folder 11/1, MS 5223, Box 10, UOR.

[109] See Withers, 'Enterprising Women'.

[110] Andrew Frayn, 'Social Remembering, Disenchantment and First World War Literature, 1918–30', *Journal of War and Cultural Studies*, 11 (3) (2018), 192–208.

of the war, it was also in part how surviving soldiers, or bereaved relations, vented frustration with the challenging political and economic climate of the late 1920s.[111]

By the time of Virago's republication of Brittain's *Testament of Youth* in 1978, the disillusioned narratives associated with First World War remembrance had become a widely available storytelling structure that stretched across generations; a vehicle through which public mourning was permissible, intelligible and repetitious.[112] The diffusion of remembrance as social literacy and sensibility – a mode of reading tragedy and trauma at the interstice of the world-historical, public and private, personal and political – informed what became, through the 1979 BBC series and a Fontana paperback tie-in, the second coming of *Testament of Youth*'s mass-market success. Brittain's memoir resonated as a personal account of the war, no doubt. 'If you enjoyed the television series, get the book. If you didn't, get it anyway. It is inspiring reading', wrote Liz Hartley in *Spare Rib*, in January 1980.[113] *Testament of Youth* had further resonance in the late 1970s, however, because it offers a record of how more or less ordinary people can survive catastrophic generational and political change. On the surface, the late 1970s seem to have little in common with conflicts of the Edwardian era. It was a time, however, riven with economic and social uncertainty, due to systemic restructurings connected to deindustrialization and a dramatically shifting, if contingent, ideological climate. In this context, Brittain's *Testament of Youth* became part of a range of socially available cultural discourses, a resource through which feelings about emergent, and not-yet-comprehensible historical change, could be channelled. From *Testament of Youth* I turn to another Virago republication that converged with remembrance culture: Rebecca West's *Return of the Soldier*. Published as a VMC in 1980, the novel was also adapted for screen – this time cinema – and published by Fontana as a mass-market paperback. *Return of the Soldier* had nowhere near the same cultural impact as *Testament of Youth*; indeed,

---

[111] Mark Bostridge, *Vera Brittain and the First World War* (Bloomsbury, 2014), 124–6.

[112] Daniel Todman, *The Great War: Myth and Memory* (Continuum, 2005), 221–2.

[113] Liz Hartley, 'Review of Testament of Youth', *Spare Rib*, 90 (1980), 48.

both film and tie-in were comparative commercial 'flops'. The book none-theless enables further consideration of how Virago's reprint publishing traversed the cultural and affective field of remembrance.

3.1 Testament of Youth

Vera Brittain has, for literary critic Jane Potter, 'become for the general reader the token "woman's voice" of 1914–18 . . .. Her memoir, *Testament of Youth*, which expresses the disillusionment of the interwar period, speaks to our twenty-first-century sensibilities, scarred by a Second World War, Vietnam, Bosnia, the "war on terror", and other numerous national and international conflicts.'[114] Yet Brittain's book has not always been a fixture of the cultural landscape. For those of feminist and pacifist sensibility in the 1960s and early 1970s, to read Brittain's memoir meant spending 'the odd shilling on a mouldering copy' in second-hand shops or borrowing it from a library. When Virago republished the memoir in 1978, the book that had been out of print for nearly two decades became again the 'very latest thing'.[115]

Testament of Youth, like many books Virago republished, was recom-mended by an Advisory Committee member. Rosalind Delmar, one of many scholars and intellectuals connected to the WLM who Virago drew on for advice, lent Callil a copy of the book as a holiday read.[116] Bostridge offers a vivid picture of Callil 'sitting, reading it, on Melbourne's Elwood Beach . . . moved to tears, and returned to Britain determined to republish'.[117] Such resolve brought rich commercial rewards for Virago. These extended far beyond unit sales which, in themselves, were

---

[114] Jane Potter, *Boys in Khaki, Girls in Print: Women's Literary Responses the Great War 1914–18* (Oxford University Press, 2008), 1–2.

[115] Glastonbury, 'When Adam Delved and Eve Span'. For reference to reader demand for *Testament of Youth* in libraries, see Carmen Callil to Mark Shivas, 19 July 1977, Add MS 89178/1/7, BL.

[116] Future VMC were often holiday reads for Callil. References to such practices are numerous within the Virago and Carmen Callil archives, held at the British Library.

[117] Bostridge, *Vera Brittain*, 159.

substantial: published in April 1978, Virago's edition had sold 19,541 copies by January 1981, making it a resounding bestseller for the company at that time. Significantly, *Testament of Youth* introduced Virago to the profitability of TV tie-ins and subsidiary rights exploitation. It also opened up opportunities to republish further 'forgotten' texts written by Brittain and her contemporary, Winifred Holtby, who shared the same literary executor, Paul Berry. The immense popularity of *Testament of Youth* stimulated interest in 'what happened next' in Brittain's life and, amid 'the explosion of the Vera Brittain industry', the other *Testament*s – of *Experience* and *Friendship* – were republished.[118] In 2012, VMC status was finally conferred on *Testament of Youth*. The book has an important place in the history of Virago's reprint publishing and reveals how the cultural impact of Virago broadened in the late 1970s.

Testament of Youth certainly struck a chord with audiences and readers in the late 1970s. Publishing any successful book, as already indicated, requires establishing sensibility that a story is relevant to the contemporary moment. Publicity discourses can outline how a book converges with pressing political or cultural issues; they can also draw on time itself. The year 1978 marked the sixtieth anniversary of the end of the First World War. While certainly not an anniversary with the gravitas of a centenary or even half-century, the date signalled a recognisable point in time in which the 'commemorative impulse – the visceral need to remember the war at significant moments in time' was enacted.[119] Women's accounts of the First World War were hardly absent from the historical record, as Brittain's voluminous memoirs evidence. Nonetheless, these stories failed to achieve parity with masculine ideas of heroism, suffering and sacrifice which dominated remembrance imaginaries.

[118] Carmen Callil to Paul Berry, 10 February 1981, Add MS 88904/1/194, BL; Andrea Earney to Carmen Callil, 15 August 1978, Add MS 88904/1/194, BL.
[119] Emma Hanna, 'Contemporary Britain and the Memory of the First World War', *Matériaux pour l'histoire de notre temps*, 113–14 (1–2) (2014), 110–17. https://doi.org/10.3917/mate.113.0110#xd_co_f=OTExYTljZTgtNDI1YS00NTI1LTgwNDMtYjE5YjI1NzNhMGJh~.

Testament of Youth tells the history of Brittain's war; the centre of the book focuses on her service as a Voluntary Detachment Nurse and the loss of her fiancé, friends and brother. These intense and tragic stories are bookended by Brittain's experience at Somerville College, University of Oxford, a portrait of a precocious young woman with feminist and, later, pacifist politics.

The vernacular weight of feminism in the 1970s public sphere softened the cultural ground into which Brittain's memoir was republished.[120] Remembrance cultures, in turn, lent *Testament of Youth* a gravitas that arguably eclipsed, or absorbed, the threat of its feminism. Writing in 1986, Callil reflected, wryly, that Virago's main cultural achievement was reaching a 'general audience of women and men who had not heard of, or who disliked or even detested, the idea of feminism'.[121] Virago's women-centred, feminist publishing, in other words, worked against the grain of entrenched social and cultural taste. Due to this, the popular success of a Virago book should not be taken for granted. In the case of Brittain's memoirs, the remembrance context meant audiences could permissibly embrace the book, even if they found its feminist content, or the fact it was published by a feminist company, challenging.[122] Through Brittain's book Virago's reprint publishing was distributed across broad, affectively potent textures of historicity rooted within British society in the late 1970s. In the process, feminism's cultural influence was spread and embedded, popularised and vernacularized.

---

[120] For Bostridge (158–9), other important references are the fourth series of the BBC drama *Upstairs, Downstairs*, screened in 1974, which demonstrated the impact of the war on the Bellamy Household, and the Imperial War Museum's 1977 exhibition *Women at War, 1914–18*.

[121] Carmen Callil, 'The Future of Feminist Publishing', *The Bookseller*, 1 March 1986, 850–1.

[122] As George Caitlin, Brittain's husband reputedly did, expressing his dislike of the name 'Virago' which he associated with lesbianism. Due to this, he did not want to be associated with Virago's version of the book. See Bostridge, *Vera Brittain*, 160–1.

From early on, Callil saw potential for a TV serialisation of *Testament of Youth*. She contacted the BBC to discuss the idea in 1977, a proposition that was not taken seriously until favourable reviews of the book were published.[123] The five-part adaptation was screened in November 1979 and received wide critical praise.[124] The TV serialisation was faithful to Brittain's feminist narrative, placing, as Brittain's text does, Vera and Ronald's shared interest in Olive Schreiner's writing at the centre of their courtship. Virago had republished Schreiner's economic treatise *Women and Labour* in 1978, as part of the Virago Reprint Library (see Chapter 2). In the BBC adaptation, Vera quotes from part of the book as she and Ronald sit by a fire, locked in playful intellectual exchange. As she brushes her hair, they discuss her favourite writers. These include the familiar – and canonised – George Eliot and Emily Brontë, both of whom are absent from the parallel scene in Brittain's text.[125] The scene then cuts to Vera and Ronald taking a bracing walk on open hills near Buxton. Roland registers his surprise at Vera's adoration of Schreiner's 'strident' political text and wonders why she was not included in Vera's list of favourite novelists. Vera replies, aghast, 'I didn't realise she'd written any novels.' '*The Story of an African Farm*, you *must* have read that one', is his response.[126] Dialogue drops away as the camera focuses on their faces – Vera delighted at Ronald's winning feminist credentials; Ronald's manner betraying smug satisfaction that his niche reading habits might secure Vera's affections. This romantic, intellectual exchange presents Ronald in the image of Schreiner's 'New Man'. It is also indicative of how Virago's central marketing concept, that widened understanding of how patriarchal literary cultures are structured to forget women writers, had become

---

[123] Carmen Callil to Mark Shivas, 19 July 1977, Add MS 89178/1/7, BL; Bostridge, *Vera Brittain and the First World War*, 161.

[124] Nancy Banks-Smith, 'Testament of Youth', *The Guardian*, 5 November 1979.

[125] *Testament of Youth*, 84–5.

[126] *Testament of Youth* (1979/2010), BBC, B003EQ4Y8G. Schreiner's text was, at the time, available in paperback, published by Penguin. *Story of an African Farm* was published as a Virago Modern Classic in 1989.

broadly meaningful. Adapted from the WLM's 'Hidden from History' maxim (see Chapter 2), this notion was vernacularized and recognisable *enough* to be a cultural reference point in the late 1970s. The scene dramatizes Vera's surprise when she learns about a corpus of feminist writing she had no idea existed, a revelation akin to a moment of wonder. Her gait conveys the political potential and pleasure of (re)discovery, positioning such curiosity as an intimate connection between personal and literary desire. It was a scene repeated in bookstores and libraries in Britain from the late 1970s onwards, as book buyers and readers turned toward texts Virago republished and recognised their cultural value in this dual sense: The feeling that 'I didn't know about them, but I should' became a form of distinction, a social orientation to the printed and bound written word, that augmented the 'Classic' designation bestowed on the reclaimed writer.

The success of the BBC's *Testament of Youth* gave Virago further opportunities to exploit rights held in the book. In 1979, Callil negotiated a deal with Fontana to publish a limited licence mass-market paperback in association with Virago.[127] This deal enabled Callil and her colleagues to learn more about the industry, especially with regard to contract negotiations. Writing to friend and US-based literary agent Ginger Barber in 1979, Callil revealed: 'as the years have gone by, and I have learnt more, I've constantly changed the contracts to give me more control of the books, so with each book the situation is different!'[128] The Fontana deal provided concrete experience of how to make money from the business of books.[129]

---

[127] Lennie Goodings, *A Bite of the Apple* (Oxford University Press, 2020), 27.

[128] 'Carmen Callil to Ginger Barber, 5 Oct 1979', MS 5223 Box 10, File 11/1, UOR.

[129] Antonia White's *Frost in May* was another TV series/mass-market partnership between Virago and Fontana. In 1982, a two-volume *Frost in May* was published to coincide with the BBC four-part series based on White's novels, *Frost in May*, *The Lost Traveller*, *The Sugar House* and *Beyond the Glass*. Critics anticipated the series would 'become as important a piece of television drama as Vera Brittain's *Testament of Youth*'. Geoffrey Wansell, 'Chilling View of Catholic Control', *The Times*, 14 May 1982, 16.

Fontana was one of a number of publishers established in the 1950s (Pan, Corgi and Panther were others) that published cheap paperback books, aimed at the mass market.[130] During Virago's development as an independent company in the late 1970s, they were advised by friend and industry-disruptor Paul Hamlyn to side-step this form of publishing and instead sell rights for key titles to mass-market publishers who catered for readers different to Virago's core audience.[131] Hamlyn's recommendation, like many others he offered to Virago during the period when the company grew in the late 1970s and early 1980s, proved prescient with regard to Brittain's *Testaments*.[132] Further Fontana deals for *Testaments of Experience* and *Friendship* followed, while US-based Seaview published a hardback version of *Testament of Youth* in 1980, and Wideview produced paperback versions of all three titles the following year.[133] 'The sales figures I attach will show just how much good you and Vera have done for Virago', Callil exuded to Berry, appending royalty cheques for rights and sales of Brittain's titles in March 1981.[134] Priced at £1.75 (compared to Virago's version, which sold at £2.95 when first published, increasing to £3.95 by 1984), the Fontana's *Testaments* quickly sold over 100,000 copies, benefitting from Fontana's wider distribution in high-street and railway stores. By the end of 1980, the combined sales of Fontana and Virago editions of *Testament of Youth* totalled 223,364 (home) and 11,142 (export), with combined sales of *Testament of Experience* amounting to 114,051 (home) and 2,936 (export).[135]

Importantly, Fontana sales did not detract from the sale of Virago's versions. Indeed, Brittain's *Testaments* were key profitable titles during the

---

[130] Iain Stevenson, *Book Makers: British Publishing in the Twentieth Century* (British Library, 2010), 154–6.

[131] 'Notes on meeting with Paul', Add MS 89178/1/8, BL.

[132] Withers, 'Enterprising Women'.

[133] Virago would later sell paper rights for books they originally published, such as Zoe Fairbairns's historical saga *Stand We at Last* (1983), published by Pan Books, April 1984.

[134] 'Carmen Callil to Paul Berry 10 March 1981', Add MS 88904/1/194, BL.

[135] 'Vera Brittain: Testaments – Sales to 31 12 80', MS 5223 Box 10, File 11/1, UOR.

late 1970s and early 1980s. Along with another film tie-in, Miles Franklin's *My Brilliant Career*, they 'really kept the company going since June [1980]'.[136] After a disappointing – and chaotic – sales and distribution relationship with Wildwood that resulted in poor stock and financial management, early in 1980 Virago enlisted Sidgwick & Jackson as sales representatives.[137] As Griffin explained in a letter to the new sales representatives:

> Many people will want to buy these as a set and only Virago will be able to supply this (not a boxed set, but three volumes alike in format and design). *Our editions are better bound and altogether more attractive than the Fontana ones* and, as you will see from the sales figures I'm sending you next week, despite the availability of the Fontana *Testament of Youth*, ours has sold extremely well. Booksellers sometimes need to be convinced that the two editions can, and do, sell side by side.[138]

By January 1981, after being on sale for just under three years, Virago's version of *Testament of Youth* had sold 19,541 copies. By March 1982 sales of the book had increased by over 50 per cent to 31,470.[139] Within the context of other Virago reprints of the era, this was a clear best-seller. By April 1980, the top selling VMC were Antonia White's *Frost in May* with 11,401 copies and Stevie Smith's *The Holiday* with 7,525 copies. Bestsellers from the Virago Reprint Library were *Round About a £1 a Week* (10,201 copies) and *Life as We Have Known It* (7,033 copies). At this time, other

[136] 'MONEY/FINANCIAL CONTROLS etc', MS 5223 Box 10, File 11/1, UOR.

[137] See MS 5223, Box 12, University of Reading for evidence of how Kate Griffin and Harriet Spicer attempted wrestle control of Virago sales and distribution from Wildwood; Sidgwick & Jackson carried the stock from July 1980 and started to officially sell from 1 September 1980. 'Notes on Sidgwick Meeting', MS 5223, Box 11, UOR.

[138] 'Kate Griffin to Virago Sales Reps, 7 May 1980', MS 5223, Box 11, UOR.

[139] 'Sales Figures, March 1982'.

reprints – across the Virago Reprint Library and the VMC – rarely broke 5,000 copies in terms of sales, averaging around 3,000 copies each. In the period between 1978 and 1982, Virago really began to capture new reading markets. Griffin noted to her new sales representatives that sales and subscriptions for Virago's titles were rising all the time; she also made it clear that Virago had high expectations of the Sidgwick & Jackson team – failing to expand their market reach was not an option.[140]

While Virago's version sold well next to Fontana editions, perhaps attractive to the buyer who desired a more durable, culturally distinct edition, the difference in sales figures (which is between hundreds of thousands and tens of thousands) is, nonetheless, striking. Despite this huge variance in figures, the Virago brand has become indelibly connected with the cultural of memory of Brittain's text. It is Virago's recovery act that has endured, an intervention that now circulates as a kind of cultural common sense, beyond the bare fact of book unit sales.[141] This is understandable: the small print of all Fontana copies clearly stated they were published in association with Virago. The tie-in was also short term and time limited, so when the license expired, Virago's were the only editions available.[142] Nonetheless, Virago's invention of a market for a new category of cultural goods – grounded in the emotional and intellectual revelation that there are forgotten women writers who you *should* know about, but don't – was, through Brittain's text, forcing its way into the mainstream.

Republishing and popularising the forgotten woman writer was an act of what Mukti Khaire calls 'pioneer entrepreneurship': the creative and visionary capacity of an individual or company to make a world in which it becomes possible for certain cultural products to be embraced by a wide range of consumers.[143] This world-making aspect of pioneer entrepreneurship has profound implications for social and cultural change, realised when cultural conditions are established that support the 'broad acceptance of the new conventions of value and criteria of

[140] 'Kate Griffin to Virago Sales Reps, 7 May 1980'.
[141] Todman, *The Great War*, 101–3. [142] Goodings, *Bite of the Apple*, 27.
[143] Khaire, *Culture and Commerce*.

quality'.[144] These processes occur through 'discursive repositioning and framing' which 'downplay or cast in a positive light those features that are most threatening or unappealing to a majority of customers'.[145] Virago's publishing wrenched feminism and women's rights from the frame of disgust and political ridicule. Republishing transformed the abjection of forgetting into the pleasure of rediscovery; the reframing of lost feminist books into desirable cultural objects was a powerful world-making action. Yet the broadening success of Virago's reprint publishing was only possible because it was densely connected to *a priori* receptiveness within a cultural field structured by heterogeneous ideas – and feelings – about the past. With Brittain's *Testaments*, Virago's reprint publishing could reach and *touch* the mass market; the emotional lives of a nation calendrically, symbolically and ritualistically shaped by remembrance. The decision to republish *Testaments* was a threshold moment for Virago. It triggered their gravitation from the niche to the popular, the terrifying to the tantalising, a site of cultural liquidation which transformed how women's writing was broadly consumed, and digested. The traumatic impact of the First World War concerns another book republished by Virago that is the focus of the next section: Rebecca West's *The Return of the Soldier*, which became a VMC in 1980.

3.2 Return of the Soldier

In her introduction letter to Virago's new sales reps in May 1980, Griffin informed the group that Rebecca West's first three novels – *The Return of the Soldier* (first published 1918), *The Judge* (1922) and *Harriet Hume* (1929) – were to be published that July. It would be the first time West's novels were widely available in trade paperback format. Of the three titles, only *The Return of the Solider* had been available in paperback in Britain, a mass-market edition, published by the New English Library in 1970. West should, Griffin anticipated, 'become as popular' as other bestselling VMC authors, Antonia White and Stevie Smith.[146] By March 1982, *The Return of the Soldier* had sold 5,819 copies, *The Judge* 5,308 and *Harriet Hume* 5,132, numbers that would have made a solid

[144] Ibid., 29. [145] Ibid., 39. [146] 'Kate Griffin to Virago Sales Reps, 7 May 1980'.

contribution to Virago's annual turnover. All books had initial print runs of 7,000, indicating Virago understood how to balance copies printed with projected sales.

West had not veered as far from the public consciousness as some writers Virago republished. Indeed, West arguably benefitted from a mini-renaissance in the mid-1970s. In 1977 *A Celebration*, a compilation of her fiction and non-fiction writing, was published by Macmillan. She had supervised filming for a TV adaptation of her novel, *The Birds Fall Down*, and continued to flex her journalistic muscles, producing a 'continual flow of highly original book reviews for the *Sunday Telegraph*, written with all the vigour of a woman of 90'.[147] West, who died on 15 March 1983, had eccentricity, wit and, most of all, staying power. She embodied the stretch across feminist generations and expressed her endurance with cantankerous flair. West emblematised the mutating ideological sands of the post-war period, a point captured by filmmaker Jill Craigie who noted how, across her lifetime, she 'fell from grace in the eyes of socialists', became conservative with a 'small c' and viewed 'ideologies as transient, for ever changing with circumstances'.[148] Despite her profile, West's corpus of fiction and non-fiction writing was not widely available at the time Virago decided to republish it. She claimed to be 'electrified' when Goodings wrote with news she had been chosen, along with Rosamond Lehmann, as one of the top twenty living British authors in a promotion activity organised by The Book Marketing Council. 'For many years', West hushed, 'there was a sort of conspiracy of silence about my work.'[149] Inclusion in the promotion meant Virago books would, for the first time, get 'into areas in which we are usually considered too specialist or "high-brow"', Goodings explained to West, such as W.H. Smith or John Menzies.

---

[147] Jill Craigie, 'The Times Profile: Dame Rebecca West, 90 Years Old This Month'. *The Times*, 6 December 1982, 8.

[148] Jill Craigie, 'The Times Profile'.

[149] 'Correspondence Between Rebecca West and Lennie Goodings, 16–17 November 1981', Add MS 88901/1/439, BL. Goodings also recounts this story in her memoir. See Goodings, *Bite of the Apple*, 69.

As interest in West's works increased in the early 1980s, hardback publishers became aware of a valuable asset lurking on their backlist. At the end of 1970s, Virago paid between £400 and £750 for *The Return of the Solider*, *Harriet Hume* and *The Judge*. When it became apparent there was a new market for West's writing, the cost of securing rights began to spiral. In late November 1982, Mary Pachnos, rights manager at Macmillan, wrote to Owen with news that paperback rights were available for *The Fountain Overflows* and *The Thinking Reed*.[150] In a remarkable stroke of naivete, Pachnos explained that West's novels were now very popular due to rising interest in women's writing. The letter is annotated in biro by a Virago staff member with an (understandably) exasperated response: 'What an idiotic letter!'[151] Callil's initial offer for *The Fountain Overflows* and *The Thinking Reed* was £750. To her surprise, she became embroiled in a bidding war with Penguin, who counter-punched with an offer of £1,750. Callil's highly identifiable handwriting is scrawled across the letter announcing Penguin's bid: 'Frame this!'[152] Eventually the bidding concluded; Virago paid Macmillan £15,250 advance for the books, against royalties of 7.5 per cent home and 7.5 per cent export, rising to 10 per cent home and export after 30,000 copies sold.[153] In the space of only a few years, the value of West's writing had inflated significantly against the wider recognition of 'women's writing' as market category.

The feminist reception of Virago's publication of West's novels was less enthusiastic. *The Return of the Solider* tells the story of Chris,

---

[150] These titles had most recently been available in paperback in 1979 through Pan, Macmillan's mass-market imprint.

[151] 'Mary Pachnos to Ursula Owen, 25 November 1982', Add MS 88901/1/440, BL.

[152] 'Mary Pachnos to Carmen Callil, 13 December 1982', Add MS 88901/1/440, BL.

[153] Mary Pachnos to Carmen Callil, 23 Dec 1982', Add MS 88901/1/440, BL. Virago would continue to be asked to pay high prices for West's works. See also 'Mary Pachnos to Carmen Callil, 11 May 1984', Add MS 88901/1/439, BL, informing her that rights were now available for *The Birds Fall Down* and *This Real Night*.

a soldier who is injured while on duty and returns home shell-shocked. Chris's traumatic experience causes him to flee the present and retreat to an innocent, happier, adolescent state; a stranger from himself and the historical time to which he returns. Around Chris are three women – Kitty, his wife; his cousin Jenny, narrator of the story; and Margaret, Chris's first love and teenage sweetheart, whose working-class background adds texture and tension to West's narrative. Pam Johnson, writing in *Spare Rib*, criticised the female 'parasitism' and male idolatry present across all three novels. The class attitudes dramatised in *The Return of the Solider* also acted as a 'serious obstacle to the full enjoyment of West's work'. While West portrays Margaret in a positive light, as the only character who can liberate Chris from his mnemonic stupor, she was – according to the *Spare Rib* reviewer – at best idealised and, therefore, distanced from reality.[154] The visceral, engrained prejudice of social class in Britain is, indeed, brutally exposed in West's novella. Jenny, the main narrator of the story, confesses she 'hated [Margaret] as the rich hate the poor', seeing her as comparable to 'insect things that will struggle out of the crannies which are their decent home, and introduce ugliness to the light of day',[155] 'spreading stain on the fabric of our life'.[156] The violence of West's language – arguably intending to expose rather than endorse such prejudice – may well have jarred against the political sensibilities of an 'incipient' feminist criticism, cultivated in the pages of magazines like *Spare Rib* and others.[157] Virago's publishing at this time, amid the thrust of market creation, nevertheless began to

---

[154] Pam Johnson, 'Review of *The Return of the Soldier*, *The Judge* and *Harriet Hume*', *Spare Rib*, 101 (1980), 42.

[155] Rebecca West, *The Return of the Solider* (1918; Virago 2010), 20.

[156] West, *Return*, 23.

[157] See also Janice Winship's analysis of reviews in *Spare Rib*, which discuss how cultural products were rated or rejected depending on their 'incipient' feminist criteria. Janice Winship, *Inside Women's Magazines* (Pandora, 1987), 139. For a rigid critical assessment of Brittain's *Testament of Youth*, viewed through an incipient feminist lens, see Maroula Joannou, 'Vera Brittain's *Testament of Youth* Revisited', *Literature & History*, 2 (2) (1993), 46–72.

outstrip its initial audience base of readers, tied to the political interests of the WLM. Throughout society, more readers turned toward books written by 'reclaimed' women writers, informed by the everyday art of feminist literary-critical literacy popularised by Virago's marketing concept.[158]

Like *Testament of Youth*, the meaning of *The Return of Soldier*, when republished in 1980, was contextualised by the remembrance cultures that emerged after its initial 1918 publication. While the dominant tone of *Testament of Youth* is centred on grief, loss and mourning, *The Return of the Soldier* is defined by its eerie, temporal dislocation, released through the narrative inscription of trauma, a 'strangeness [that] had come into the house and everything was appalled by it, even time. For the moments dragged.'[159] It is through such dragging – temporal drag, to invoke Elizabeth Freeman's term, a sense of being suspended in a contingent, unknown, paralysing time/space – that *The Return of the Solider* connects to the uncertain spirit of the late 1970s and early 1980s.[160] A time that did not know itself; shell-shocked historicity, psychic life stuck in perpetual delay, retreating from the agony of a present defined by economic, political and cultural flux. We encounter these symptoms (again) through *The Return of the Solider*'s dramatization of trauma's complex temporalities. Centred on different layers of trauma experienced by the characters, social relations are trapped in lived temporalities that are incommensurable but, nonetheless, coeval. In this sense West's story creates a therapeutic space within which trauma, as a state of being that

[158] For an example of how Virago's publishing was reviewed in non-feminist publications, and how feminist content was subject to a different set of valuation criteria, see Patricia Beer's review George Gissing's *The Odd Women* and Sarah Grand's *The Beth Book* from the *London Review of Books*, 17 July 1980. Praising the former over the latter, the political 'single-mindedness' of Grand was viewed by the reviewer to be 'much less persuasive' than Gissing's 'ambivalence'; she recommends that the two books be read in parallel 'by anyone wanting a demonstration of the difference between a tract and a novel'. Patricia Beer, 'New Women', *London Review of Books*, 17 July 1980.

[159] West, *Return*, 39.

[160] Elizabeth Freeman, *Time Binds: Queer Temporalities, Queer Histories* (Duke University Press, 2010).

dislocates and is dislocated within time, is treated and reckoned with.[161] When first published in 1918, such meaning would have clearly resonated with direct experience of the First World War. Republished during the early years of Margaret Thatcher's tenure as prime minister, the story's presentation of techniques that reconcile trauma's temporal dislocations add further layers to its therapeutic function. The narrative arc is constructed to bring characters 'back' to live together, albeit ambivalently, within a ruined historical time. This sensibility resonated with how with the advent of Thatcherism was experienced by those on the left, and certainly by those with feminist sympathies, but it also had a broader relevance for those coming to terms with the transformed social, economic and moral landscapes of post-industrial society.

Tantalised, one suspects, by the success of the BBC adaptation of Brittain's first *Testament*, *The Return of the Solider* was made into a film that was released in January 1983. It was one of three British entries to the Cannes Film Festival in May 1982, an ambitious promotion activity backed by the British Overseas Trade Board with the intention to showcase the British film industry.[162] While the film was lauded for its 'touching fidelity' to the novel, most reviews were lukewarm.[163] *The Return of the Soldier* is an early example of what would later in the decade be critically dismissed as 'heritage film'. Set in an elegant country house with 'careful period décor, luscious pastoral landscapes', the film is composed in slow-paced, soft-focused shots that linger equally on characters and interior design.[164] The heritage film critics of the late 1980s would likely have argued that the film advanced the Conservative Party's cultural agenda. This, they suggested, aimed to promote public

---

[161] Steve Pinkerton, 'Trauma and Cure in Rebecca West's *The Return of the Soldier*', *Journal of Modern Literature*, 32 (1) (2008), 1–12.

[162] Made by Skreba Films, a production company set up by Ann Skinner in 1978, there were several challenges during production, including loss of funding. Leslie Geddes-Brown, 'The Real-Life Drama Behind the Film', *The Sunday Times*, 16 May 1982; David Robinson, 'Cinema', *The Times*, 25 May 1982, 13.

[163] David Robinson, 'Passionate Paradoxes', *The Times*, 7 January 1983.

[164] 'London,' *The Times*, 8 January 1983, 7.

acceptance of the propertied classes as core to Britain's national interest and values.[165] When the film was released in early 1983 however, the cultural discourse surrounding heritage film had not yet been fully defined, so such criticisms were absent. Hazy aesthetic tropes dominate in the film; these accentuate the story's suspension of temporality and desire to turn back the clock to an innocent, happier time. Characters often appear in front of mirrors, suggestive of split temporal existence, straddling multiple pasts and contingent presents. This Lacanian twist on a quintessentially Freudian tale offers cultural space in which the subjects' struggle to recognise themselves – and the symbolic times they live in – are objectified, put on display, through the moving cinematic image. In this sense, the 'strangeness' that in West's original novel 'had come into the house' so that 'everything was appalled by it, even time', is remediated in the socio-political context of the early 1980s.[166] The film interpolates the viewing audience as 'inhabitants of this new tract of time' where the 'sky also is different', a difference that is felt psychically and affectively, but not yet fully understood.[167]

Virago knew, from experience, that significant profits could be made through licensing titles to mass-market paperback imprints, especially when a film or television tie-in was involved. For *The Return of the Soldier*, Virago would again partner with Fontana to produce the book. The results, this time, were less rewarding. Partly this was a consequence of poor timing. In a letter to Simon King of Fontana, written by Owen on 4 October 1982, she expressed concern that Fontana had released their version of *The Return of the Soldier* the previous week, three months before the release of the film on 6 January 1983. Virago's contract with Fontana stipulated they were to publish their version to coincide with release. Due to this contract breach and its likely adverse impact on sales, Owen wrote to Fontana to ask for compensation.[168] On 31 October 1984, Susan Watt from Fontana wrote to Owen with news that overstocks of

---

[165] Claire Monk, *Heritage Film Audiences: Period Films and Contemporary Audiences in the UK* (Edinburgh University Press, 2011), 11.

[166] West, *Return*, 39. [167] Ibid., 43, 45.

[168] 'Ursula Owen to Simon King, 4 Oct 1982', Add MS 88901/1/440, BL.

Fontana's edition of the book were to be remaindered, confirming the anticipated poor sales.

Inefficient scheduling cannot solely be blamed for the poor sales of this Fontana paperback; as established from reviews of the film, *The Return of the Soldier* did not 'break' the mass market.[169] Even so, by the end of 1984 Virago's publishing – and the wider market category of 'Women's Writing' – arguably had. At this time, Virago had navigated their evolution from being a small independent, entrepreneurial firm, publishing for well-defined, committed audiences, to reach a broader cohort of readers. One explanation for this remarkable transition lies in how the books Virago reprinted, such as Brittain's *Testaments* and West's *The Return of the Soldier*, touched widely held historic structures of feeling that have, in the aftermath of the First World War, organised the nerve centres of British culture and society. The mnemonic message of both texts – their capacity to reflect on and manage catastrophic grief, dramatic historical change, trauma and temporal delay – amplified and accelerated as they intersected with the audio-visual flows of television and cinema. This meant that the cultural intervention that propelled Virago's recovery publishing was reinforced in vernacular, everyday contexts which, in turn, shaped widespread reading, buying and publishing practices. The final chapter turns to my last sense of the past that Virago's reprint publishing converged with: Heritage.

---

[169] 'Susan Watt to Ursula Owen, 31 Oct 1984', Add MS 88901/1/440, BL.

4 Heritage

> I thought, I'm going to start a fiction list, and I'm going to make the
> books look gorgeous so everybody will want to read them.[170]

'A hundred years hence,' Brittain imagined, 'literary tourists will find in
Yorkshire the opportunity for many pious pilgrimages.'[171] Rambling
across the rugged landscape and the county's towns and cities, she exuded
cultural confidence that future visitors will flock to the area to pay respect
to her contemporaries: Phyllis Bentley, Storm Jameson and good friend
Winifred Holtby, the subject of her third 'Testament' – *of Friendship* –
first published in 1940. Sounding like a contemporary National Trust tour
guide, Brittain encourages the reader to visit the village of Rudston, 'first
in late summer, when a golden glow of grain ripe for harvest lies over the
wheat fields beneath the huge open vault of the sky and its slowly
marching pageant of cloud'.[172] For those who visit Holtby's grave,
a host of sensory pleasures awaits them. It is an ideal place to listen as
'the quiet air gradually fills with innocent country sounds – the lowing of
cows, the throb of a reaping-machine in the valley, the sudden call of
a blackbird, the soft chirping of invisible larks.'[173] A beautiful scene;
saturated with pastoral imagery that stirs a desire to visit and value the
untarnished splendour of the English landscape set apart – culturally – by
the literary brilliance cultivated there. Finally, we complete the pilgrimage
and reach Holtby's grave. Stopping here, Brittain imagines the literary
tourist 'will copy the short black-lettered inscription' carved onto the
headstone that reveals Holtby's life was 'yet briefer . . . than her country-
woman Charlotte Brontë, whose frail life was extinguished at the age of
thirty-nine'.[174] This handwritten, mid-twentieth-century memento would
likely take the form of an Instagram post for the 'pilgrims of the twenty-
first century', a cohort Brittain reaches out to, in this future-orientated
tourist map.[175]

[170] Callil in *The British Book Trade*, 213.
[171] Vera Brittain, *Testament of Friendship* (1940; Virago 2012), 7.
[172] Brittain, *Testament of Friendship*, 9. [173] Ibid., 9. [174] Ibid., 10. [175] Ibid., 8.

A little more than forty years later, a memo lands abruptly on the desks of sales manager Kate Griffin and marketing manager Lennie Goodings, in Virago's Wardour Street offices. The pair had recently sent Callil an outline of publicity and promotion plans for Virago's 1982 titles. Their strategy is to consolidate Virago's presence in towns and cities outside of London, targeting places with universities and good bookshops, such as Norwich, Southampton and Sheffield. The hope is to emulate the 'successful attack' that took place in Oxford the previous year, which led to Virago's titles being stocked in all bookshops in the city.[176] Callil, however, was not so impressed with the plans. Why was there not any focus on the places depicted in Virago titles, or the towns and cities where authors were born and had lived? The 'local author angle' had been pursued successfully the previous year, with 7,000 two-colour leaflets distributed during the 'Shropshire celebrations' to mark Virago's publication of three novels by Mary Webb – *Precious Bane*, *Gone to Earth* and *The House in Dormer Forest*. Callil had even written 'What about Winifred?' in response to a sales conference report in January 1981, bemoaning the lack of focus on marketing opportunities in Yorkshire. It was as if Brittain had been whispering in her ear.[177]

Callil was open with her colleagues about being 'hampered as you both obviously are by my lack of knowledge of English Geography'. She nevertheless committed to the idea that local marketing was an effective way of communicating the literary value of Virago's books. She quickly offered the following suggestions:

Buckinghamshire: I know nothing about Buckinghamshire (check with Harriet) BUT

- a) Rosamond [Lehmann] was born there
- b) May Sinclair died there and lived there from 1932 till her death in 194– something

---

[176] 'Notes from Lennie and Kate's Publicity/Promotion Meeting on 28 January 1982', Add MS 89178/1/45, BL. For an illuminating account of Virago establishing relationships with booksellers in Oxford, see 'Notes on Oxford Visit to Blackwells', MS 5223, Box 10, File 11, UOR.

[177] 'Sales Conference Notes – 15 January 1981', MS 5223, Box 10, UOR.

c) Elizabeth Taylor. Every single novel she wrote is set (I think) in Buckinghamshire. Check with Alexandra [Pringle] too. She lived in Penn Bucks, or was [it] High Wycombe? And that is the world of her novels, down to the last pub?

I've no idea if there are any good bookshops in this area.[178]

In this communication, Callil's sense that marketing narratives can be usefully combined with a place-based heritage narrative is pronounced emphatically.[179] Literary tourism and heritage was hardly a new cultural phenomenon in the early 1980s.[180] As noted above, the practice was depicted vividly in the opening pages of Brittain's tribute to Holtby and, even now, her time-travelling paean feels remarkably contemporary in how it conveys the entwined value of literature, personality and landscape. By the early 1980s, heritage – as an aesthetic, commercial and social practice – had seeped into the lived environment; the conservationist impulse sculpted the habitus of every-day and political life, no longer the 'preserve of aesthetes or of minority groups or campaigners, as it had been in the earlier days of preservation'.[181]

Heritage plaques were the means through which literary distinction was amplified in publicity: 'author work: Elizabeth Taylor was born in Reading: Media and bookshop promotion. Is there a plaque possibility here?'[182] Often, it turned out, there were few plaques celebrating Virago authors. Due to this, Virago entered the heritage fray in 1984 with their own 'Virago Green Plaque' competition. The competition was only open to booksellers and riffed on the blue plaque scheme, established in 1866, which honoured historic sites where

---

[178] 'Memo from Carmen Callil to Kate Griffin and Lennie Goodings, Regarding Their Publicity Notes for Virago Press Titles', Add MS 89178/1/45, BL.

[179] Later in her memo, Callil does concede that Goodings' and Griffin's plans to reach out to regional bookshops were, in fact, well founded. Callil's manage-ment style could be idiosyncratic, improvised and at times confrontational. See Goodings, *Bite of the Apple*, 28–36.

[180] Nicola J. Watson, ed., *Literary Tourism and Nineteenth Century Culture* (Palgrave, 2009).

[181] Samuel, *Theatres*, 237.

[182] 'Virago Press Marketing Schedule 1982', Add MS 89178/1/46, BL.

distinguished people – rarely women – lived and worked. Entrants were tempted with a cash prize of £100 and were invited to find a house in Britain and Ireland where a VMC author had lived. If the house was empty and the owner agreed, a green plaque was positioned outside it.[183] In 1984, Virago Green Plaques were positioned on houses related to Radclyffe Hall, Harriet Martineau and Sheila Kaye-Smith. Adorned with the company's bitten apple and proud statement: 'Radclyffe Hall, 1880–1943. Novelist. Lived Here.'[184]

Heritage is the third and final 'sense of the past' to be investigated in this Element. Doing so will elaborate another temporal-historical dimension through which Virago's reprint publishing was recognised, valued and adopted by readers.[185] This chapter is primarily concerned with the aesthetics, design features and material properties of the VMC, a curatorial and marketing project that did not only recover the women's literary past, but re-covered it. I analyse how the convergence of Virago's late 1970s and early 1980s publishing with photo-setting technologies enabled the company to produce books that not only recirculated the typeset aesthetics of previous eras, but also rematerialised cultural value, previously embedded in hardback editions, in handheld paperback form. In this sense, the VMC produced in the late 1970s and early 1980s enacted an aesthetic democratisation, eroding cultural access to literary distinction within 'an aura of pastness' implanted in their photo-set, trade paperback.[186] Finally, this chapter will consider how Virago's reprint publishing ran on parallel tracks to Thatcher's invocation of 'Victorian Values', arguing it offered an Other way to access the literary, cultural and political heritage of the nineteenth century: through its resurrected feminist writers.

4.1 Covers

VMC are renowned for how they recovered women's literary heritage. To do this effectively, Virago's publishing moved beyond discerning practices

---

[183] 'Where Are All the Blue Plaques Celebrating Women?' www.virago.co.uk/virago-news/2019/02/20/where-are-all-the-blue-plaques-celebrating-women/. Last accessed 30 March 2020.

[184] 'Virago Green Plaque Competition Flyer 1985', Add MS 89178/6/45, BL. The competition also ran in 1985.

[185] Samuel, *Theatres of Memory*, 15. [186] Ibid., 113.

of selection and organisation, their books were also re-covered; repackaged in a smart formalisation of 'retro-chic' aesthetics that had, by the late 1970s, marched from the margin to the centre of the cultural taste. Samuel observed 'retro-chic's 'feminine aspect', and wondered if it was connected to the increased economic influence of women, as workers and earners, in the post-war period.[187] In this light, it is tempting to view VMC, as well as Virago's success and the wider market recognition of women's writing, as indicative of how the cultural sphere underwent a substantial feminisation in the late twentieth century, an era in which public life became amenable to feminist ideas through their wide dispersion – and consumer adoption – in symbolic life. Virago's design aesthetic converged with and reflected popular visual tastes grounded in a disposition to heritage; this smoothed the passage of the publisher's books as they locked into mainstream cultural flows. The series was conservative, not in the political sense, but in its aim to conserve a tradition of women's writing. In this way Virago's activities struck a chord with the wider social environment that was playfully, proudly and enthusiastically ensconced with history as pastime and mass activity, history as symbol and spectacle.[188] Much like Samuel, I do not see social and cultural practices aligned to 'Heritage' as always already vapid or reactionary, especially when the concern is the construction and conservation of tradition centred on the work of writers whose cultural presence is marginalised due to engrained structural attitudes that discriminate on the grounds of race, gender, class, sexuality and so forth.

Indeed, Virago's artful re-covering of its Modern Classics – a series that importantly classified living, contemporary authors within its frame – was a vital factor in *how* the books became lodged into and, in turn, sculpted social space. As a 'symbol' that caught 'the mood of the time', they were how 'Virago entered the public consciousness – and stayed', notes Goodings.[189] This is true, demonstrably, but still: what were the social conditions that supported the rebounding of women's literary achievements in the book-buying environments of the late 1970s and early 1980s? In what ways were such milieu primed to be responsive to the aesthetic presentation of the VMC? How were the everyday environments constituted by a novel

[187] Ibid., 98.   [188] Samuel, *Theatres*, 25.   [189] Goodings, *Bite of the Apple*, 72.

relationship to the past that supported readers to pass positive judgement on an otherwise displaced cultural object: a forgotten, neglected woman author?

Books are always judged by their covers and new readers can be drawn to familiar visual codes. Like any successful book cover, the VMC benefitted from inhabiting a dual space. The design was created by Mick Jarvis, then deputy art director at mass-market paperback house Panther.[190] It was distinctive but cleverly echoed existing, popular and recognisable design concepts. VMC adapted the 'Marber Grid' used to compose Penguin book covers since the early 1960s and specifically modelled on Penguin's Modern Classics of the late 1960s–early 1970s. From the Penguin Modern Classics they 'borrowed' the idea of reproducing paintings on the front cover, taking advantage of late twentieth-century advances in industrial scale, four-colour off-set printing.[191] The chosen images occupied three quarters of the jacket and were selected in order to best convey the mood and atmosphere of the novel, invocating literary sense and sensibility. Dark green was (now famously) chosen for the background – a neutral colour space that for Callil broke apart the colour-coded binarisms of blue masculinity and pink femininity.[192] The series title appeared in a light green smaller font and headlined the cover; author and book title were presented in a larger font. All three were boldly aligned to the sinister left rather than right, as Penguin Modern Classics were from the late 1960s onward, encouraging reorientation of the arm, hand and eye as they reached towards the book.[193] This appropriation of

---

[190] Callil, *The British Book Trade*, 213. In terms of spatial composition, VMCs were left-aligned like Panther's late 1960s 'Crimeband' series. Callil would likely have been familiar with this design because she worked for the company in the late 1960s. For examples, see Kurt Weidemann, *Book Jackets and Record Sleeves* (Thames and Hudson, 1969), 162–3.

[191] Goodings, *Bite of the Apple*, 74; Greg Neville, 'How the Marber Grid Was Made', 2017, https://penguinseriesdesign.com/2017/02/15/how-the-marber-grid-was-made/. Last accessed 24 March 2020.

[192] Callil, *The British Book Trade*, 213.

[193] Henry Eliot, 'Designing Penguin Modern Classics (Part 1)', www.penguin.co.uk/articles/2017/penguin-modern-classics-design-part-1.html.

known form, transformed through subtle compositional differences grounded in colour and spatial emphasis, embedded the VMC within the familiar palette of existing book design while setting apart the series' original – and singular – message; a home for all those 'foot-off-the-ground novel[s] that came by the left hand'.[194]

Choosing an appropriate image to grace the cover was a vital part of the books', and the series', visual message. Callil, Pringle and later Lynn Knight, sourced images. These came mostly from regional, national and independent galleries throughout Britain, with some acquired from institutions internationally, after initial discovery in exhibition catalogues, auction guides or gallery visits.[195] The book cover design of the VMC was of crucial importance because it became the platform from which Virago's wider publicity strategy was built. VMC enabled Virago to create striking publicity iconography that extended their territorial presence within bookshops and, consequently, wider society. Virago's success here echoes Penguin's march into public space in the 1930s through the use of mascots and 'branded' publicity that encouraged booksellers to create special displays that showcased Penguin books.[196] With the VMC, though, Virago had numerous 'mascots': the faces of authors featured in the series adorned postcards and posters, readily distributed by the company and often displayed by supportive booksellers.

Even so, resistance to the VMC's feminine heritage aesthetic was sometimes encountered. In December 1981, Griffin wrote to Mr G.F. Cousins, manager of Leicester University Bookshop, berating him for not displaying any of the twelve VMC posters Virago had sent. These featured authors such as Radclyffe Hall, Rosamond Lehmann, Antonia White, Christina Stead, and others. If he were to do so, Griffin wrote irreverently, he should inform the

---

[194] Stevie Smith, *Novel on Yellow Paper* (Virago, 1980), 38.

[195] Add MS 89178/1-129-155, BL, contains all the receipts for Virago's business activities between 1977 and 1981, including many from galleries from which Virago leased cover images.

[196] Richard Hornsey, '"The Penguins Are Coming": Brand Mascots and Utopian Mass Consumption in Interwar Britain', *Journal of British Studies*, 57 (4) (2018), 812–39. https://doi.org/10.1017/jbr.2018.116.

Figure 2 Virago Modern Classics Poster Elizabeth Taylor, Add MS 89178/6/53, British Library © Virago.

Virago sales rep as 'it would make her day'. Cousins replied, dismissively, informing Virago's buccaneering sales manager that, for any such poster to be displayed, the author must have recognisable literary excellence and, if not

Figure 3 Virago Modern Classics Poster, E. Arnot Robertson, Add MS 89178/6/53, British Library © Virago.

that, a very distinct face. Edith Sitwell, he relayed churlishly, only qualified on account of the latter, rather than the former. Griffin resolved to have the final word: 'I think they all have rather interesting faces. Henry Handel

Richardson in particular almost rivals Edith Sitwell (whose poetry I must admit to loving as much as her eccentricity).'[197]

This is not the only example of the friction Virago sometimes experienced in their attempt to claim prime retail space in bookshops.[198] In April 1980, members of Virago attended a Booksellers Association conference in order to better understand how to reach readers and influence booksellers. They noted: 'we don't spend a lot on promotions etc and it was obvious that many booksellers don't know us or our books very well yet. They're also a bit frightened of our image ... we had to get the message across that we're not ferocious and terrifying.'[199] 'We actually had to charm the [retail] book trade', remembered Griffin. 'We had to become friendly with them. We had to demonstrate that the books would sell, that we ... wouldn't just put the books in their bookshops and expect them to do all the work .... We would activate the market to go into the bookshops. That's not the language we used then, but ... that's what we did.'[200] This was especially true among 'provincial' booksellers who perceived Virago as a specialist feminist press and, therefore, not suitable for their shops.[201]

[197] 'Correspondence Between Kate Griffin and Mr G.F. Cousins, 23 November– 1 December 1981', MS 5223, Box 11, UOR; the full Virago Modern Classics poster set can be found at Add MS 89178/6/53, BL.

[198] Booksellers also refused to stock Virago's books, such as the university bookshop in Aberdeen run by a Catholic manager who disapproved of the publication of *Make It Happy*; another bookshop in Inverness did not order Virago's books because they believed they would not sell. 'Kate's Notes from Scottish Trip 15–17 July 1981', MS 5223, Box 11, UOR.

[199] 'BA Conference – Fri 18th–Monday 21st April', MS 5223, Box 10, File 11/1, UOR. Emphasis in original.

[200] Kate Griffin interview by D-M Withers (2020), The Business of Women's Words: Purpose and Profit in Feminist Publishing, British Library Sound & Moving Image Catalogue, reference C1834/17, © The British Library.

[201] 'Preliminary Notes on Booksellers Conference', Folder 11/1, MS 5223, Box 10, UOR. It was around this time that Virago decided to remove the statement 'VIRAGO is a feminist publishing company', followed by this Sheila Rowbotham quote, from the front of their publications: 'It is only when women start to organize in large numbers that we become a political force, and begin to

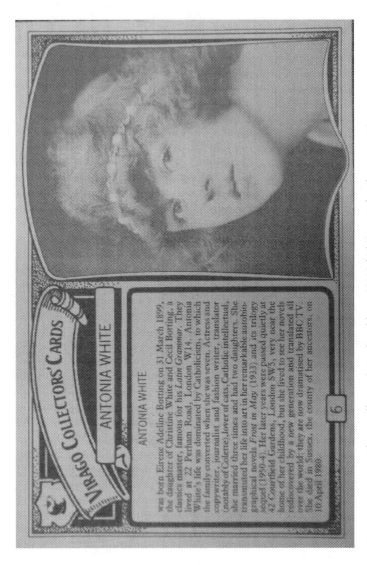

Figure 4 Antonia White Collectors' Card, Add MS 89178/6/42, British Library, © Virago.

VIRAGO COLLECTORS' CARDS

REBECCA WEST

REBECCA WEST

was born Cicily Isabel Fairfield in London on 21
December 1892. The daughter of a Scottish mother
and an Anglo-Irish father, she spent her childhood in
Edinburgh. A feminist and a radical, she found her
true vocation when she was 19: she became a
journalist on the *Freewoman* and Blatchford's *Clarion*.
Bernard Shaw said of her 'Rebecca can handle a pen as
brilliantly as ever I could, and much more savagely'.
This wit and genius can be seen in all the works of this
formidable woman of letters: she has written novels,
biography, history, satire, travel and criticism. Her
only child, Anthony West, by the writer H.G. Wells,
was born in 1914. For 38 years she was married to
Henry Maxwell Andrews and they lived in
Buckinghamshire. Dame Rebecca West (she was
honoured in 1959) lives in London and continues to
write and be what Bernard Levin has called 'the
greatest English [sic] woman since Elizabeth I'.

5

Figure 5 Rebecca West Collectors' Card, Add MS 89178/6/42, British Library, © Virago.

From 1981 onwards, Virago increased their efforts to reach booksellers and new readers through substantial investment in attractive marketing materials. The twelve VMC author posters, which used the format of book covers to frame portraits of featured writers, were part of a specifically dedicated VMC promotion planned for June/July 1981. Virago also produced a full-colour leaflet featuring all VMC jackets, which included an order form and space for a bookshop's stamp. Catalogues, paper and carrier bags were made available to booksellers for free. Green-coloured VMC branded 'spinners' were budgeted for in 1980 but, eventually, deemed too expensive, even though booksellers began to ask repeatedly for such marketing paraphernalia. At this time VMC branded 'dumpbins' were created instead. In May 1982 a series of six Virago author 'Collectors' Cards', that included author photographs and a brief biography, were created. These were numbered to appeal to the collector's instinct and designed in the style of celebrity collector's cards, used by tobacco companies of the late nineteenth and early twentieth centuries to market cigarettes as a 'cool', desirable product. The first six starred Antonia White, Rebecca West, May Sinclair, Charlotte Mew, Ada Leverson and Rosamond Lehmann.[202]

Many booksellers responded enthusiastically to these materials, using author posters and book jackets to create window displays with elaborate, wallpaper backdrops which honoured local authors.[203] In Greenhead Books, then a new bookshop situated in a Leeds shopping mall, a Virago display filled one window, with a celebration of Charles and Diana's marriage in the other. Ensuring Virago books were in the *right* space in bookshops was also important. In a letter to a bookseller working for James Thin, Edinburgh, informing them that two VMC 'dumpbins' would be sent

move towards the possibility of a truly democratic society in which every human being can be brave, responsible, thinking and diligent in the struggle to live at once freely and unselfishly.'

[202] 'Notes on Virago Meeting 29.10.80', MS 5223, Box 10, File 11/1; 'Kate Griffin to John Keegan 1 May 1981', MS 5223, Box 11, UOR. See also Add MS 89178/6/46, BL, for VMC marketing materials.

[203] 'Kate Griffin to Ann Pritchard, 28 July 1981', MS 5223, Box 11, UOR. The author in question was Stevie Smith.

for use in their shops, Griffin asked, suggestively: 'Will you put them in the Penguin part, or in with the other mass market paperbacks?'[204] Such nudges were common in her correspondence with booksellers, inviting them to imagine how Virago's marketing materials could be best positioned in order to capture the attention of the lurking consumer. There is no doubt that the VMC were decisive in easing Virago's passage into the mainstream; as early as 1979 sales reps noticed the series was 'splitting' the backlist, with earlier Virago books stocked in radical bookshops, while the VMC were able to reach into more 'middle-of-the-road' territories.[205] This trend continued apace, partly due to the unified design of the books which enabled titles to be logically displayed together. The series was recognisable with a striking solidity, especially when presented alongside a wealth of marketing paratexts that further distributed the aesthetic sensibilities that bound the series together throughout social space.

Outside the bookshops, Virago's VMC, sporting their famous green spines, acquired distinct social meaning. This cut through gendered distinctions too, as Goodings comments in her memoir: 'I know men who say they kept a VMC by their bed to show women how intelligent, enlightened and thoughtful they were.'[206] While this may have been a strategic act of product placement, it also conveys how Virago's publishing contributed to the malleability of social space in the 1970s and 1980s, feminising the palette of literary taste, breaking down gendered reading distinctions, especially those rooted in the denigration of the feminine.[207] It was the VMC that helped secure the affections of Virago's most consistent and influential financial supporter, the printing entrepreneur Robert Gavron, who first expressed his admiration for the series after Callil sent him copies of *Frost in May*, *Mr. Fortune's Maggot* and *The True Heart* to read in 1978.[208] Appealing

---

[204] 'Kate Griffin to Alan Boyd, 28 July 1981', MS 5223, Box 11, UOR.

[205] 'Kate Notes on Sales Conference', MS 5223, Box 10, File 11/1.

[206] Goodings, *Bite of the Apple*, 62.

[207] Janice Radway, *Reading the Romance* (University of North Carolina Press, 1984).

[208] 'Letter from Bob Gavron to Carmen Callil, 23 June 1978', Add MS 89178/1/9, BL. At the time Gavron provided business and financial advice to Virago and

to the taste of rich, powerful men and massaging the social digestion of feminist ideas among an emergent business elite were important elements in Virago's success; from this flowed meaningful and sustained investment in their enterprise.[209]

For those who grew up after the creation of the VMC, the books acted as an important feminist reference point. Sociologist Carly Guest's personal reflection on how she became a feminist in the 1980s tells us this, describing how the process was cultivated by 'pulling a Virago or Women's Press book from my grandmother's bookshelf and reading, the bottle green and black and white striped spines such a *familiar* and *enduring* signifier of feminist writing'.[210] In this sense, the VMC 'green spines' commanded a literacy of their own. When situated in social space, they changed how that social space was 'read'. Another writer recalls that seeing Virago titles on her mother's friends' bookshelves communicated feminist aspirations: 'I had no idea what these authors actually wrote, but, in a sense, I knew just from what I observed from their owners' who were 'the kind of women I wanted to be when I grew up: learned, eloquent, slightly bohemian, generous of spirit, but firm in their convictions.'[211] Green spines acted as building blocks of a feminist habitus, instating tiny monuments of feminist presence within domestic space. As a collection, unified through a marketing aesthetic, they spatially embedded feminist literary heritage in the social environment.

4.2 Interiors

The VMC, as cultural objects that carried untimely authors into the path of mass-market readership in the late 1970s were, paradoxically,

had, along with Paul Hamlyn, acted as guarantor for the bank loan that enabled Virago to become an independent company in 1976. From 1987 onward, Gavron was Virago's main investor until the sale of the company to Little, Brown in 1995. See Withers, 'Enterprising Women'.

[209] See Withers, 'Enterprising Women'.

[210] Carly Guest, *Becoming Feminist: Narratives and Memories* (Palgrave, 2016), 207. My italics.

[211] Johanna Thomas-Corr, 'Fiery Women', *The Sunday Times*, 23 February 2020, 33.

a material product of their time. The adoption of new technological methods in the 1960s printing industry shaped the interior feel and look of Virago's reprint publishing. Phototypesetting, also known as photo-composition, was a photo-mechanical system coordinated by the leader of post-war technology, the computer. Flexible and adaptive to different sized operations, phototypesetting could effectively be combined with offset lithography printing and, by the end of the 1960s, was used throughout the industry for a wide range of setting work.[212] While printing firms adopted different forms of photocomposition during the 'White Heat' decade of technological progress, they

> all worked on the same basic principle of setting type by photographing characters on film from which printing plates were made. The characters were then developed as photographic positives on film or light-sensitive paper from a negative master containing all the characters; the film, carrying the completed text, would then be used for making a plate for printing.[213]

Virago's VMC were 'shot' from the original, hardback publications; they transformed imprinted hot-metal set text into photographed characters in a momentary flash of light. Computer-coordinated photocomposition, when matched with offset lithography, was an extremely disruptive technology within the printing industry, and broke with 'centuries-old techniques of casting and letter-assembly, heralded as a new conception of type composition'.[214] Through its erosion of craft labour and automation of procedures carried out, historically, by the skilled labourer's hand, computer-aided photosetting feminised (and therefore devalued) composition. It was, rather curiously, 'setting type without type', a process through which the mechanical world straddled the digital simulacrum.[215] Photosetting was used

---

[212] Alan Marshall, *Changing the Word: The Printing Industry in Transition* (Comedia, 1983), 40.

[213] Bromage and Williams, 'Materials, Technologies and the Printing Industry', 47.

[214] Marshall, *Changing the Word*, 40.   [215] Ibid., 40.

in the printing industry for a relatively short period of time. By the mid-1980s, these methods were superseded by rapid advances in computerisation, leading to the digitisation of all aspects of production, from text setting and word-processing to the use of optical character recognition. This means, though, that the specific form of the first-generation of VMC are imprinted with the marks of an important window in post-war British technological history; a time when technologies used in key industries were hybrid, modular constructions, neither fully mechanical, nor fully electronic. Attending to this technological complexity, especially with regards to print, enables better understanding of how the digital simulacrum generated by widespread digitalisation became material reality – as the transition and contact points between relief type, exposed film and digital media are charted. Such movement entails a slowing of historical senses down, returning to the production history of first-generation VMC in order to think again what their hybrid interior texts mean, rather than explaining such meaning away with quick reference to surface and aesthetic appearances.

The VMC were certainly an outgrowth of what Samuel characterised as the 'retro-chic enthusiasms' of the 1960s. These 'self-consciously *minority* tastes' were driven by the 'historical instinct' of the collector, who foraged in flea-markets and antique stores in search of the latest old thing.[216] Virago spent significant resources researching – and searching for – potential VMC titles. They pursued many different avenues to access women's literary heritage, including public, university and subscription libraries, as well as benefitting from generous reader recommendations. Second-hand bookshops, and the skilful detective work of book-finders, were vitally important for the realisation of the series.[217] After Virago acquired rights to publish from the hardback publisher, author, or their literary executors, the best quality copy was used to produce the interior of the new Virago edition. Seller lists from second-hand booksellers offered succinct instructions that

---

[216] Samuel, *Theatres*, 92; 113. Italics in original.

[217] For detailed discussion see D-M Withers, 'Virago Modern Classics: The Making of a Reprint Series', in *The Edinburgh Companion to Women in Publishing, 1900–2000*, ed. Nicola Wilson et al. (Edinburgh University Press, forthcoming).

would guide Virago's canny purchases: D.M. Prall had two copies of Storm Jameson's *No Time Like the Present*, one 'VG/excellent but d/w slight torn & slightly fingermarked'. Graham K. Scott, bookseller had one copy of *The Tortoise and the Hare* Gollancz, first edition, 1954, 'binding soiled & rubbed but sound (ex-WHS Liby.) Clean internally'.[218]

Good quality books were not always easy to find, and rights-holders did not always have a suitable copy on file. Books with irregular histories, like Rebecca West's *The Judge*, out of print since publication by Doubleday in 1922 with rights assigned to literary agency A. D. Peters Ltd in 1948, are a case in point. 'We only have one copy of the *The Judge* which we got by canvassing second hand bookshops, and we'll need that should you allow us to publish', Callil explained to A. D. Peters Ltd's Michael Sissons, who asked if he could view Virago's copy before granting rights.[219] On other occasions, the only available version was a mass-market paperback, like a Corgi production of Winifred Holtby's *The Crowded Street* from 1976, lent to Virago by Paul Berry, her literary executor. Due to the material properties of the cheaper mass-market paperback it was not suitable for reproduction, and Berry struggled to think of someone who might have a hardback copy.[220] Scarcity only ever fuelled, however, the clear cultural and business rationale for Virago's reprint publishing. Callil knew from experience that good quality, affordable versions of the books Virago popularised were hard to find. In the face of such rarity, Virago's main challenge was to stimulate demand and market the books, elegantly and effectively.

The VMC were not only reprints, they were copies fashioned from mechanical and light-sensitive processes that reanimated memories of the hardback past within a trade paperback container. Since the late nineteenth century, elite cultural commentators had stoked fears about the degradation of literary taste that they viewed as the consequence of rapid

---

[218] 'Receipts from September 1981', MS 5223, Box 1, UOR.

[219] 'Carmen Callil to Michael Sissons, 26 Jan 1979', Add MS 89178/2/80, BL.

[220] 'Correspondence Between Carmen Callil and Paul Berry, 27–31 Aug 1980', Add MS 88904/1/194, BL.

advances in print industrialization.[221] The unique composite trade paperback, pioneered by Virago with the VMC, therefore, materially broke
down forms of distinction that culturally separated hardback and paperback formats on the grounds of value, prestige and taste. It also rode
roughshod through material distinctions that maintained hardback and
paperback publishers as 'rigorously segregated species' in the publishing
industry – a tradition that would be rendered obsolete with the invention
of 'vertical' publishing the following decade.[222] The materiality of this
literary composition was one important, tactile element through which
Virago accommodated popular tastes to untimely women writers, and
previously indigestible feminist ideas. This publishing practice represented a democratisation, rather than degradation, of the reading public.
Such cultural levelling applied, of course, to the proclaimed aim of the
series, to reclaim women's literary heritage. Yet it also inhered in the
book's material form, which cut through engrained and restraining forces
of aesthetics and taste which, in turn, reproduce cultural logics of disgust
and exclusion.

To understand the erosive, cultural impact of the VMC in the late 1970s
and early 1980s, the material properties of the book must be considered.
This retro was not simply a surface, all too easily associated with a vacuous,
Laura Ashley-style, middle-class aesthetic. It had depth, secreted between
the pages of the book, a relation between then and now that reached out to
the reading eye and from which each reader could decode their own
position within multi-valent historical time. 'Because all the Virago
Modern Classics were offset from their original productions', Virago editor
Ruthie Petrie remembers, 'it meant the variety in type and in size of type
and in readability, legibility and so on, varied hugely from book to book to

---

[221] Anthony Enns and Bernhard Metz, 'Distinctions that Matter: Popular
       Literature and Material Culture',*Belphégor*, 13–1 (2015), http://journals
       .openedition.org/belphegor/606; https://doi.org/10.4000/belphegor.606
       . Last accessed 16 March 2020.

[222] Stevenson, *Bookmakers*, 178–9. Stevenson traces the erosion of separate practices
       for hardback and paperback publishers to the actions of Tony Godwin who
       created a hardback imprint within Penguin, which became Allen Lane in 1967.

book.'[223] While these unique design features were noted fondly by Virago editors, Petrie remarked that she was unsure if *the reader* ever noticed. Yet, given the uniformity of Penguin and Faber productions at the time, she speculated, it is certainly possible they did recognise the difference. Decades on from its republication by Virago, I reach for the nearest green spine on my bookshelf – George Egerton's *Keynotes & Discords*, published 1983. The gaping margins and setting in large, Caslon font are most definitely legible in this composite oddity (a double composite, since when originally published *Keynotes* and *Discords* appeared as separate volumes). In contrast, the mid-century publication of Stevie Smith's *The Holiday*, first published 1949 and republished by Virago in 1979, has tighter margins but generous space for thumbs. But the trace of the other typeset is discernibly there – a trace of the Other typeset historical time. The coexistence of different temporalities within the single book is communicated via such font variations; the economical, condensed now of introductions frame the larger, perhaps lucid, declaration of then. A different edition transported – remarked – in time.

VMC did not hide the fact that the 'new' book was composed from other publications. The story of the forgotten book invoked its own story. The copyright page offered clues – 'first published by', 'Virago edition offset from first British editions' – rough edges of past texts coexisted; not smoothed out, flattened down or obscured in search of 'brand consistency'. Rather, this sense of the past – the tactile time-travel which let Other historical times and a suppressed textual heritage flood in – *was* the brand. Late twentieth-century destabilisations in historical perspective, especially in relation to authenticity and 'truth', are often viewed as the outcome of postmodern theorisations. Rarely are the mass circulation of reprints considered to contribute to the dislocation of normative historical 'reality' in the late 1970s and early 1980s. Yet such texts did much to provide evidence that challenged the assumed historical and literary position of women. That sense of: was it really like that? Did women in the past actually live, feel and

---

[223] Ruthie Petrie interview by D-M Withers (2018), The Business of Women's Words: Purpose and Profit in Feminist Publishing, British Library Sound & Moving Image Catalogue, reference C1834/02, © The British Library.

speak like that? But there, reproduced in the VMC was the material proof –
a trace, photo-lifted from the past, 'function[ing] as a technology of cultural
memory, shaping our historical consciousness'.[224]

VMC were literary and aesthetic emblems of an 'expanding historical
culture, in which the work of inquiry and retrieval is being progressively
extended into all kinds of spheres', propelled, in this instance, by the
commercial success of reprinted feminist books.[225] This emergent social
literacy, that extended how the past within the present was 'read', and
circulated the idea that books had their own, often perilous, neglected history,
became woven into cultural valuation practices. Paul Foot's introduction to
Schreiner's *From Man to Man*, republished by Virago in 1982, remarked that
when he had 'finished my 1927 edition (*third impression*) . . . [I] reflected sadly
that it would only reach the few in my generation who scour through second-
hand bookshops, or who are lucky enough to find it in a library'.
Furthermore, he presses, the title 'went into at least three editions after
Olive's death, then vanished into obscurity from which I beg some lively
publisher (why not Virago?) to rescue it'.[226] In this introduction, bibliographic information is not viewed as a peripheral, or even a scholarly concern.
Foot's framing indicates how we are to read – indeed position – Schreiner's
book: within the historical context of the early 1980s, where understanding of
'tradition' is conditioned by an emerging, quotidian awareness of a book's
publishing history. Present in Foot's text is the intellectual feeling Virago
popularised – the wonder of discovery, the deep wish and desire for the
*re*discovery of neglected books – against the backdrop of scarcity: the
dusty second-hand shop or the postcode lottery of the municipal libraries.

The bibliographic became an important element of Virago's marketing
discourse too. Potted publishing histories were a staple of Advance
Information Sheets, compressed into purposeful soundbites, easily recallable
by sales reps and booksellers. *Aurora Floyd*, published in Virago's Victorian

---

[224] Kate Mitchell, *History and Cultural Memory in Neo-Victorian Fiction* (Palgrave, 2010), 13.
[225] Samuel, *Theatres*, 25.
[226] Paul Foot, 'New Introduction' to Olive Schreiner, *From Man to Man* (Virago, 1982), xvii.

Classics series in August 1984, was the 'first one-volume edition since 1890s, first paperback edition'.[227] George Eliot's *Brother Jacob*, published July 1988, was available 'on its own for the first time – previously published in a 1878 Cabinet Edition, together with *Silas Marner* and *The Lifted Veil*'.[228] Such publicity discourse synthesised cultural and economic value in a way that positioned the book and its history in the marketplace. The publication of a 'famous' woman writer like George Eliot in the VMC is symptomatic of the transformation of the series towards the end of the 1980s; as VMC matured, its marketing message became absorbed by the publishing establishment. A memo from Callil in May 1987 emphasised the importance of gaining better financial returns from the series, exploiting its positive reputation, brand recognition and hard-won space in bookshops.[229] There were also changes in how the series were framed for the reader: by 1988, introductions which outlined an unknown author's literary or feminist credentials were deemed superfluous. Introductions were instead to be produced in-house, conveying basic autobiographical facts, with the suggestion they could even be dropped entirely.[230]

The VMC developed amid the changing historical sensibilities of the 1980s. In January 1983 Margaret Thatcher made her famous reference to 'Victorian Values' which became 'one of the defining moral concepts of Thatcher's premiership' and reconfigured the Victorian age as the heyday of free

---

[227] 'Aurora Floyd, Advance Information Sheet', Add MS 89904/2/17, BL.

[228] 'Brother Jacob, Advance Information Sheet', Add MS 88904/2/11, BL.

[229] Virago had not however conquered *all* bookselling spaces. In a report from a trip to library suppliers and bookshops in Scotland, likely from 1986, Pringle told colleagues that the library market in Scotland was resistant to Virago, even though they bought trade and mass-market paperbacks. While wholesalers denied that Virago's low sales resulted from political dislike, Pringle was not convinced. This resistance may not have been about feminism alone, it could also have been underpinned by national and class-based perspectives. 'Report from Alexandra Pringle Discussing Her Visit to Scottish Booksellers and Authors, November [no year]', Add MS 89178/1/115, BL.

[230] 'Memo from Carmen Callil to Alexandra Pringle, 26 February 1988' and 'Memo from Carmen Callil to Alexandra Pringle and Lynn Knight, 7 May 1987', Add MS 89178/1/112, BL.

Figure 6 Virago Modern Classics 1982 Catalogue Cover, Add MS 89178/6/ 46, British Library © Virago

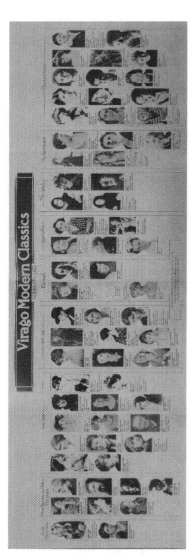

Figure 7 Virago Modern Classics 1983 Catalogue Insides, Add MS 89178/6/46, British Library © Virago

enterprise, discipline, self-reliance and family values.[231] Samuel argued that Thatcher's invocation resonated with the voting public because of disenchantment with 1960s modernisation; he also pointed to the widespread 'transformations in the perception of past–present relations' which drew 'subliminal strength from the revival of period styles'.[232] Did the VMC contribute to this 'subliminal strength' as they claimed space in bookshops, and passed into the hands of increasing numbers of readers? Perhaps.[233] By 1982, the series was clearly marketed as a 'heritage brand': these 'outstanding series of 19th and 20th century novels' were 'rediscovered classics of our literary heritage'.[234] The choice of Britannia, pensive and engrossed in a Modern Classic, as emblem and marketing mascot for the series in this period brought together ideas about national and cultural heritage with combative – yet protective – imperial maternal power that had penetrated the social imaginary.

Virago had drawn on the imagery of Britannia before: she appears on the cover of the 1976 publication *The Women's Directory*. Across its early period, the concept of women's literary heritage constructed by Virago was clearly racialised white and situated in a (post) imperial frame. The first Caribbean author published in the VMC was Phyllis Shand Allfrey in 1982. That same year, Paule Marshall became the first African American author featured in the series with *Brown Girl, Brownstones*, originally published in 1959.[235] Further African American authors followed, with Zora Neale

---

[231] Jessica Prestidge, 'Housewives Having a Go: Margaret Thatcher, Mary Whitehouse and the Appeal of the Right Wing Woman in Late Twentieth-Century Britain', *Women's History Review*, 28 (2) (2019), 277–96, https://doi.org/10.1080/09612025.2018.1482656.

[232] Samuel, 'Mrs. Thatcher's Return', 12–14.

[233] Owen commissioned journalist and political activist Beatrix Campbell to write *The Iron Ladies: Why Do Women Vote Tory?* in 1987, a book viewed as central to the historiography of Conservative women in the twentieth century. See Julie V. Gottlieb and Beatrix Campbell, 'The Iron Ladies Revisited', *Women's History Review*, 28 (2) (2019), 337–49, https://doi.org/10.1080/09612025.2018.1482660.

[234] 'Virago Modern Classics Catalogue 1982', Add MS 89178/6/46, BL.

[235] During a visit to the Frankfurt Book Fair in the late 1970s, Virago attempted to acquire books written by West Indian authors, perhaps intended for its reprint

Hurston's *Their Eyes Are Watching God* published in 1983 and Ann Petry's *The Street* in 1986. Such books were published to time with the huge popularity of contemporary African American authors like Pulitzer Prize winners Alice Walker, published by The Women's Press in 1983, and Toni Morrison, published by Chatto & Windus since 1979. The charismatic Maya Angelou, whose autobiography *I Know Why the Caged Bird Sings* was accorded VMC status in 2012, became an immediate bestseller for Virago when published in 1984. The publication and promotion of contemporary Black American women writers was often criticised by Black British writers in the 1980s, who did not feel that commercially orientated, feminist publishers gave their work the same level of support.[236]

4.3 Virago Victorian Classics

It is clear Virago's publishing complemented the cultural and political ferment of the early 1980s. It was an age that had come to deeply socialise heritage values and appreciate heritage *had* value – distilling the sensory essence of the past as identity and consumer distinction. Bent towards the feminine and attentive to the curational efforts of feminist publishers, it was an environment in which Virago's publishing could take hold and *persist* in cultural space. Virago also launched their own appeal to Victorian values at this time; August 1984 saw the announcement of a new sub-series, the Virago Victorian Classics (VVC). Virago had published Victorian writers since the inception of the VMC, but this differentiation of the Classics brand curated a specific space for 'four of the late nineteenth century's most

series, but were unsuccessful. Plans to commission a biography of Mary Seacole from this time were also not realised. See 'Frankfurt Notes: Books on Offer: List Additional to Ursula's', MS 5223, Box 10, UOR. Seacole's autobiography, *The Wonderful Adventures of Mrs Seacole in Many Lands*, first published in 1857, was republished by Bristol-based feminist and socialist publishers Falling Wall Press in 1984.

[236] See Barbara Burford, ' . . . And a Star to Steer Her By', in *Charting the Journey: Writings by Black and Third World Women*, ed. Shabnam Grewal, Jackie Kay, Liliane Landor, Gail Lewis and Pratibha Parmar (Sheba, 1988), 97–9.

Figure 8 Four Great Victorians Poster, Add MS 89178/6/53, British Library © Virago

talented and prolific writers: Mrs Oliphant, Mary Braddon, Rhoda Broughton and Mrs Humphrey Ward'.[237]

This distinction applied to publicity framing only. The covers of the VVC used the same design as standard VMC and did not include a 'Victorian' rather than 'Modern' descriptor. Callil took a consultative and careful approach to researching the series, asking passionate readers for opinions to ensure the most appropriate novel was selected. This included Showalter, whose *A Literature of Their Own* had a major influence on the development of VMC, offering Virago a range of authors they might publish and providing a critical framing discourse for the series. Callil explained to Showalter that her selections for the VVC 'showed a particular tradition in women's 19th Century writing which I think connects strongly with some of the popular writers of the 20th century'.[238] In another letter Callil enthused about Mary Cholmondeley's *Red Pottage*, a book recommended to her by the critic and published by Virago in 1985, revealing that she had 'just chosen the most wonderful pre-Raphaelite painting for the cover'.[239] Aware of growing market recognition for the 'Victorian woman writer' and the period category more broadly, Callil often asked advisors to keep Virago's 'Victorian' publishing ambitions a secret. Writing in January 1982 to Tamie Watters, who penned introductions to Rhoda Broughton's *Belinda* and Mrs Humphry Ward's *Marcella*, with news that Virago planned to publish Broughton in the summer of 1984, Callil emphasised: 'Could you keep this information to yourself? I'm more than somewhat worried that someone else will pinch the idea.' This paranoid sentiment resurfaced in a letter to Mr Stock Clark, a passionate reader of Mrs Oliphant's novels, as Callil worried that other publishers might 'steal the idea'.[240]

[237] 'Virago Victorian Classics', Add MS 88904/2/17, BL.

[238] 'Carmen Callil to Elaine Showalter, 11 July 1983', 7ESG/A/02/Showalter, WL.

[239] 'Carmen Callil to Elaine Showalter 21 May 84', 7ESG/A/02/Showalter, WL.

[240] 'Carmen Callil to Mr. Stock Clark, 25 January 1982', 'Carmen Callil to Tamie Watters, 25 January 1982', Add MS 88904/2/17, BL.

After the launch of the VVC, Virago were disappointed with the coverage received in the media. This was despite energetic publicity, timed to coincide with Virago's summer reading campaign and where ideas about using commemorative plaques to publicise books were discussed for the first time.[241] Goodings wondered if limited commercial uptake could be explained by book length. The first four VVC were originally published as three-decker volumes, released simultaneously and sent out to reviewers five weeks ahead of publication – perhaps not providing enough lead time to be read by a busy reviewer. To increase the profile of the VVC and hook reader interest, Goodings suggested the series could benefit by including one of the more well-known Victorian women writers. In 1985 they did precisely this, publishing George Eliot's *The Lifted Veil* alongside *Lady Audley's Secret* by Mary Elizabeth Braddon, *Red Pottage* by Mary Cholmondeley and *The Clever Woman of the Family* by Charlotte Yonge.[242] Virago's Victorian turn was not as successful as its other Classics publishing because it potentially contradicted previously clear political messages about the recovery of women's literary heritage. Writing to Clare Colvin, in response to her review of the four Victorian Classics published in the women's magazine *Over 21*, Pringle was at pains to clarify the rationale for Virago's selection policy: 'We are publishing all different kinds of Victorian fiction,' she emphasised, 'from the overtly feminist RED POTTAGE to the conservative and moralist THE CLEVER WOMAN OF THE FAMILY ... as with all our classics, we think it important that the entire tradition of women's writing is revealed to a new generation.' Virago's Classics publishing is designed, she pressed

---

[241] 'Aurora Floyd: Advance Information Sheet', Add MS 88904/2/17, BL.

[242] 'Memo from Lennie Goodings to Carmen Callil, 4 September 1984', Add MS 89178/1/112, BL. While Virago were disappointed initially with the commercial recognition they received for the Victorian Classics, they made connections with academic departments, such as the Victorian Studies Centre at the University of Leicester, which provided advice about existing courses focused on the Victorian period. See 'Serena Maude to Joanne Shattock, 18 December 1984' and 'W. H. Brock to Serena Maude, 20 November 1984', MS 88904/2/17, BL.

further, to 'help us uncover our heritage [... and] give the most the marvellous picture of women's lives in different decades and centuries'.

In this letter, Pringle adopts a defensive tone. This is underlined in her closing statement which apologies for didacticism but, nonetheless, stresses she 'can't bear to feel that you might be under any misapprehension' as to what the true meaning of the Classics, Victorian or otherwise, are. Pringle's response suggests that by the mid-1980s, the social meaning of heritage was shifting as it became more clearly identified with a conservative political and cultural project.[243] VVC – and indeed all Virago's Classics publishing – are always to a degree subversive because they recover women writers and centre women's stories. Yet VVC, in the aftermath of Thatcher's appeal to Victorian values, signified political ambiguity. Virago's Classics had morphed into the ideological fault lines of British society where they no longer seemed out of place but were, instead, apparent as a sign of the times. The VVC may have blurred the political coherency of the series' marketing message, even as it drew conceptual strength from an idea of heritage as connected to tradition, security and greatness. In a nationalist frame, notions of tradition and heritage fuelled political fantasies and conservative rhetoric; in a feminist frame heritage translated as the possibility of intractability, endurance and presence, popularising the sense that listening to silences and recovering what has been omitted can be both pleasurable consumer activity and a modest political gesture.

---

[243] 'Alexandra Pringle to Clare Colvin, 23 August 1985', MS 88904/2/17, BL.

5 Postscript

Virago's enduring publishing and cultural achievement was to weave a noble
sense of the untimely into the business practice of publishing, and the reading
habits of consumers in the late twentieth and early twenty-first centuries. This
built-in untimeliness, designed by Callil's preference for flawed novels that
drop in and out of fashion, altered the consciousness of how readers read, and
publishers publish.[244] It established a cultural opening through which the
books 'that surprise, the ones that don't fit, that are always a bit out of
sync ... the contradictions that engage us so powerfully' became recognised,
and valued.[245] Ironically, perhaps, it is the fact that books written in a different
time and place are *of their time* that makes them flawed: sometimes saturated
with racist language and anti-Semitic stereotypes that appal and repel contemporary readers.[246] Even so, reprint publishing thrives in feminist publishing today. There is the ornate resilience of Persephone Books (established
1999), the meticulously researched publications of academic/trade crossover
publisher Handheld Press, the cutting-edge feel of Silver Press reprints and the
historical curation that shapes the British Library's Women Writers series.[247]
The year 2018 marked the fortieth anniversary of VMC, and the series
continues to be at the forefront of Virago's publishing today. The prevalence
and continued market success of feminist-leaning reprint publishing confirms
what one of Virago's great favourites mused, that 'always there are these
under-tugs and cross currents, nothing is simple, nothing to be settled'.[248]

[244] Listen to Callil discussing her flawed selections on *Backlisted*, 80, 'Elizabeth
Jenkins – *The Tortoise and the Hare*', 26 November 2018, www.backlisted.fm/
episodes/80-elizabeth-jenkins-the-tortoise-and-the-hare.

[245] Elaine Showalter in Roszika Parker and Amanda Sebestyen, 'A Literature of
Our Own', *Spare Rib*, 78 (1979), 29.

[246] Evident in this discussion with former Virago editor Alexandra Pringle about
Margaret Kennedy's *The Constant Nymph*, *Backlisted*, 113, 'Margaret Kennedy –
The Constant Nymph', 8 June 2018, www.backlisted.fm/episodes/113-margaret-
kennedy-the-constant-nymph.

[247] See www.persephonebooks.co.uk/; www.silverpress.org; www.handheldpress
.co.uk/; https://shop.bl.uk/collections/british-library-women-writers.

[248] Smith, *The Holiday*, 130.

Bibliography

Archival Sources

The British Library

'Minutes of Virago Meetings, 28 September 1973–8 January 1974.' Archive file: Add MS 89718/1/2.

'Statement from Carmen Callil.' Archive file: Add MS 89718/1/2.

'Money Problems.' Archive file: Add MS 89718/1/4.

'Carmen Callil to Mark Shivas, 19 July 1977.' Archive file: Add MS 89178/1/7.

'Company statement.' Archive file: Add MS 89178/1/8.

'Notes on meeting with Paul.' Archive file: Add MS 89178/1/8.

'Letter from Bob Gavron to Carmen Callil, 23 June 1978.' Archive file: Add MS 89178/1/9.

'Notes from Lennie and Kate's Publicity/Promotion Meeting on 28 January 1982.' Archive file: Add MS 89178/1/45.

'Memo from Carmen Callil to Kate Griffin and Lennie Goodings, Regarding Their Publicity Notes for Virago Press Titles.' Archive file: Add MS 89178/1/45.

'Sales Figures, March 1982, for Virago Press Front and Back List Titles.' Archive file: Add MS 89178/1/45.

'Virago Press Marketing Schedule 1982.' Archive file: Add MS 89178/1/46.

'Memo from Carmen Callil to Virago Press Staff Members, 13 April 1983.' Archive file: Add MS 89178/1/47.

'Memo from Carmen Callil to Ursula Owen, Lennie Goodings, Kate Griffin and Harriet Spicer, Regarding the Image of Virago Press.' Archive file: Add MS 89178/1/71.

'Virago Press Business Plan 1987.' Archive file: Add MS 89178/1/95.

'Memo from Lennie Goodings to Carmen Callil, 4 September 1984.' Archive file: Add MS 89178/1/112.

'Memo from Carmen Callil to Alexandra Pringle and Lynn Knight, 7 May 1987.' Archive file: Add MS 89178/1/112.

'Memo from Carmen Callil to Alexandra Pringle, 26 February 1988.' Archive file: Add MS 89178/1/112.

'Report from Alexandra Pringle Discussing Her Visit to Scottish Booksellers and Authors, November [no year].' Archive file: Add MS 89178/1/115.

'Carmen Callil to Michael Sissons, 26 Jan 1979.' Archive file: Add MS 89178/2/80.

'Virago Catalogue, 1975–6.' Archive file: Add MS 89718/6/2.

'Virago New Books 1977.' Archive file: Add MS 89718/6/2.

'Virago: New Books & Complete List, June 1978–June 1979.' Archive file: Add MS 89178/6/4.

Virago Press: New Books & Complete List, January 1982–March 1983.' Archive file: Add MS 89178/6/8.

'Virago Green Plaque Competition Flyer 1985.' Archive file: Add MS 89178/6/45.

'Virago Modern Classics Catalogue 1982.' Archive file: Add MS 89178/6/46.

'Virago Modern Classics Posters.' Archive file: Add MS 89178/6/53.

'Andrea Earney to Carmen Callil, 15 Aug 1978.' Archive file: Add MS 88904/1/194.

'Carmen Callil to Clare Hardisty, June 1980.' Archive file: Add MS 89904/1/194.

'Correspondence Between Carmen Callil and Paul Berry, 27–31 Aug 1980.' Archive file: Add MS 88904/1/194.

'Carmen Callil to Paul Berry, 10 Feb 1981.' Archive file: Add MS 88904/1/194.

'Carmen Callil to Paul Berry 10 March 1981.' Archive file: Add MS 88904/1/194.

'Correspondence Between Rebecca West and Lennie Goodings, 16–17 November 1981.' Archive file: Add MS 88901/1/439.

'Ursula Owen to Simon King, 4 Oct 1982.' Archive file: Add MS 88901/1/440.

'Susan Watt to Ursula Owen, 31 Oct 1984.' Archive file: Add MS 88901/1/440.

'Mary Pachnos to Ursula Owen, 25 November 1982.' Archive file: Add MS 88901/1/440.

'Mary Pachnos to Carmen Callil, 13 December 1982.' Archive file: Add MS 88901/1/440.

'Mary Pachnos to Carmen Callil, 23 Dec 1982.' Archive file: Add MS 88901/1/440.

'Brother Jacob, Advance Information Sheet.' Archive file: Add MS 88904/2/11.

'Virago Victorian Classics.' Archive file: Add MS 88904/2/17.

'Carmen Callil to Mr. Stock Clark, 25 January 1982.' Archive file: Add MS 88904/2/17.

'Carmen Callil to Tamie Watters, 25 January 1982.' Archive file: Add MS 88904/2/17.

'W.H. Brock to Serena Maude, 20 November 1984.' Archive file: Add MS 88904/2/17.

'Serena Maude to Joanne Shattock, 18 December 1984.' Archive file: Add MS 88904/2/17.

'Alexandra Pringle to Clare Colvin, 23 August 1985.' Archive file: MS 88904/2/17.

'Aurora Floyd, Advance Information Sheet.' Archive file: Add MS 89904/2/17.

University of Reading Special Collections

'Receipts from September 1981.' Archive file: MS 5223, Box 1.

'Sales Conference Notes – 15 January 1981.' Archive file: MS 5223, Box 10.

'Frankfurt Notes: Books on Offer: List Additional to Ursula's.' Archive file: MS 5223, Box 10.

'Carmen Callil to Ginger Barber, 5 Oct 1979.' Archive file: Folder 11/1, MS 5223, Box 10.

'Factors We Consider When Taking on Books.' Archive file: Folder 11/1, MS 5223, Box 10.

'Preliminary Notes on Booksellers Conference.' Archive file: Folder 11/1, MS 5223, Box 10.

'BA Conference – Fri 18th–Monday 21st April.' Archive file: MS 5223, File 11/1, Box 10.

'Kate Notes on Sales Conference.' Archive file: Folder 11/1, MS 5223, Box 10.

'Promotions Meeting 19.6.80.' Archive file: Folder 11/1, MS 5223, Box 10.

'Notes on Virago Meeting 29.10.80.' Archive folder: MS 5223, File 11/1, Box 10.

'MONEY/FINANCIAL CONTROLS etc.' Archive file: Folder 11/1, MS 5223, Box 10.

'Notes on Sidgwick Meeting.' Archive file: MS 5223, Box 11.

'Kate Griffin to Virago Sales Reps, 7 May 1980.' Archive file: MS 5223, Box 11.

'Dear [blank] from Kate Griffin, 14 May 1980.' Archive file: MS 5223, Box 11.

'Correspondence Between Kate Griffin and Mr G.F. Cousins, 23 November–1 December 1981.' Archive file: MS 5223, Box 11.

'Vera Brittain: Testaments – Sales to 31 12 80.' MS 5223 Box 11.

'Sales Figures for 1977 and 1978 Titles, Captured Jan 1981.' Archive file: MS 5223, Box 11.

'Kate Griffin to John Keegan 1 May 1981.' Archive file: MS 5223, Box 11.

'Kate's Notes from Scottish Trip 15–17 July 1981.' Archive file: MS 5223, Box 11.

'Kate's Nottingham Visit – 21st July 1981.' Archive file: MS 5223, Box 11.

'Kate Griffin to Ann Pritchard, 28 July 1981.' Archive file: MS 5223, Box 11.

'Kate Griffin to Alan Boyd, 28 July 1981.' Archive file: MS 5223, Box 11.

'Jane Gregory to Stephanie Dowrick 12 May 1976.' Archive file: CW/ 317/6.

'Correspondence Between Norah Smallwood to Carmen Callil 6–9 September 1976.' Archive file: CW/317/6.

'Carmen Callil to Jane Gregory 13 September 1976.' Archive file: UOR, CW/317/6.

University of Bristol Special Collections

'Marsha Rowe to Sheila Rowbotham, 17 October 1972.' Archive file: DM 2123/1/55.

Women's Library, London School of Economics

'Anna Davin to Sue Jessop, 17 March 1979.' Archive file: 7ADA/01.

'Anna Davin to Mrs. Bowden.' Archive file: 7ADA/01.

Sheila Rowbotham. 'The Myth of Inactivity, Ruskin College 1970.' Archive file: 7ADA/01.

Oral History Sources

Sally Alexander interview by Rachel Cohen (2012), *Sisterhood and After: The Women's Liberation Oral History Project*, British Library Sound & Moving Image Catalogue, reference C1420/45, © The British Library, The University of Sussex.

Philippa Brewster interview by Margaretta Jolly (2019), *The Business of Women's Words: Purpose and Profit in Feminist Publishing*, British Library Sound & Moving Image Catalogue, reference C1834/10, © The British Library.

Kate Griffin interview by D-M Withers (2020), *The Business of Women's Words: Purpose and Profit in Feminist Publishing*, British Library Sound & Moving Image Catalogue, reference C1834/17, © The British Library.

Ruthie Petrie interview by D-M Withers (2018), *The Business of Women's Words: Purpose and Profit in Feminist Publishing*, British Library Sound & Moving Image Catalogue, reference C1834/02, © The British Library.

Ursula Owen interview by Rachel Cohen (2011), *Sisterhood and After: The Women's Liberation Oral History Project*, British Library Sound & Moving Image Catalogue, reference C1420/36, © The British Library, The University of Sussex.

Sheila Rowbotham interview by Rachel Cohen (2010), *Sisterhood and After: The Women's Liberation Oral History Project*, British Library Sound & Moving Image Catalogue, reference C1420/10, © The British Library, The University of Sussex.

Primary Sources

BBC. (1979/2010). *Testament of Youth*. B003EQ4Y8 G.

Vera Brittain. (1978). *Testament of Youth*. London: Virago.

Vera Brittain. (2012). *Testament of Friendship*. London: Virago.

George Gissing. (1993). *The Odd Women*. London: Penguin.

Stevie Smith. (1936/80) *Novel on Yellow Paper*. London: Virago.

Stevie Smith. (1949/79). *The Holiday*. London: Virago.

Mary Webb. (1924/78). *Precious Bane*. London: Virago.

Rebecca West. (1918/2010). *The Return of the Solider*. London: Virago.

Secondary Sources

Alexander, S. (1974). The Nightcleaners' Campaign. In *Conditions of Illusion: Papers from the Women's Movement*. Leeds: Feminist Books, 309–26.

Alexander, S. (1995). *Becoming a Woman and Other Essays in 19th and 20th Century Feminist History*. New York: New York University Press.

Altick, R. (1957). *English Common Reader: A Social History of the Mass Reading Public, 1800–1900*. Chicago: Chicago University Press.

Banks-Smith, N. (1979). Testament of Youth. *The Guardian*, 5 November.

Beer, P. (1980). New Women. *London Review of Books*, 17 July.

Black, G. (2008). *Frank's Way: Frank Cass and Fifty Years of Publishing*. London: Vallentine Mitchell.

Bostridge, M. (2014). *Vera Brittain and the First World War*. London: Bloomsbury.

Bromage, S. and Williams, H. (2019). Materials, Technologies and the Printing Industry. In Nash, A., Squires, C. and Willison, I.R. eds. *The Cambridge History of the Book in Britain: Volume 7, The Twentieth Century and Beyond*. Cambridge: Cambridge University Press, 41–60.

Browne, V. (2014). *Feminism, Time and Non-Linear History*. Basingstoke: Palgrave.

Burford, B. (1988). . . . And a Star to Steer Her By. In Grewal, S., Kay, J., Landor, L., Lewis, G. and Parmar, P. eds. *Charting the Journey: Writings by Black and Third World Women*. London: Sheba, 97–9.

Burk, K. (1994). The Americans, the Germans, and the British: The 1976 IMF Crisis. *Twentieth Century British History*, 5(4), 351–69.

Cadman, E., Chester, G. and Pivot, A. (1981). *Rolling Our Own: Women as Printers, Publishers and Distributors*. London: Minority Press Group.

Callil, C. (1980). Virago Reprints: Redressing the Balance. *Times Literary Supplement*, 12 September.

Callil, C. (1986). The Future of Feminist Publishing. *The Bookseller*, 1 March, 850–1.

Callil, C. (1998). Women, Publishing and Power. In Simons, J. and Fullbrook, K. eds. *Writing: A Women's Business*. Manchester: Manchester University Press.

Callil, C. (2008). In Bradley, S. ed. *The British Book Trade: An Oral History*. London: BL Publishing, 212–13.

Callil, C. (2008). The Stories of Our Lives. *The Guardian*, 26 April. www.theguardian.com/books/2008/apr/26/featuresreviews .guardianreview2.

Caplan, J. (1977). Life as We Have Known It. *Spare Rib*, 63, 42.

Chester, G. and Nielsen, S. (1987). Introduction: Writing as a Feminist. In Chester, G. and Nielsen, S. eds. *In Other Words: Writing as a Feminist*. London: Hutchinson, 9–21.

Collini, S. (2012). 'The Chatto-List': Publishing Literary Criticism in Mid-Twentieth Century Britain. *The Review of English Studies*, 63(261), 634–63.

Collini, S. (2019). *The Nostalgic Imagination: History in English Criticism*. Oxford: Oxford University Press.

Coote, A. and Campbell, B. (1987). *Sweet Freedom*. Oxford: Blackwell.

Corder, J. and Harvey, S. eds. (1991). *Enterprise and Heritage: Crosscurrents of National Culture*. London: Routledge.

Cowman, K. (2010). 'Carrying on a Long Tradition': Second-Wave Presentations of First-Wave Feminism in *Spare Rib* c. 1972–80. *European Journal of Women's Studies*, 17(3), 193–210.

Craigie, J. (1982). *The Times* Profile: Dame Rebecca West, 90 Years Old This Month. *The Times*, 6 December.

Davies, A. (2017). *The City of London and Social Democracy: The Political Economy of Finance in Britain, 1959–1979.* Oxford: Oxford University Press.

Davin, A. (1980). The London Feminist History Group. *History Workshop Journal*, 9(1), 192–4.

Davin, A. (2000). The Only Problem Was Time. *History Workshop Journal*, 50, 239–45.

Eliot, T. S. (1945). What is a Classic? London: Faber; reprinted in Eliot, T. S. (1957). *Of Poetry and Poets.* New York: Farrar, Straus and Cudahy, pp. 53–71.

Enns, A. and Metz, D. (2015). Distinctions that Matter: Popular Literature and Material Culture. *Belphégor*, 13(1). http://journals.openedition.org/belphegor/606; https://doi.org/10.4000/belphegor.606.

Fentress, J. and Wickham, C. (1992). *Social Memory.* Oxford: Blackwell.

Firestone, S. (2015). *The Dialectic of Sex: The Case for Feminist Revolution.* London: Verso.

Foot, P. (1982). New Introduction. In Olive Schreiner, *From Man to Man.* London: Virago.

Forster, L.C. (2020). The Paris Commune in the British Socialist Imagination, 1871–1914. *History of European Ideas*, 46(5), 614–32. https://doi.org/10.1080/01916599.2020.1746082.

Frayn, A. (2018). Social Remembering, Disenchantment and First World War Literature, 1918–30. *Journal of War and Cultural Studies*, 11(3), 192–208.

Freeman, E. (2010). *Time Binds: Queer Temporalities, Queer Histories.* Durham: Duke University Press.

Geddes-Brown, L. (1982). The Real-Life Drama Behind the Film. *The Sunday Times*, 16 May.

Glastonbury, M. (1979). When Adam Delved and Eve Span. *Times Education Supplement*, 28 December.

Goodings, L. (2020). *A Bite of the Apple.* Oxford: Oxford University Press.

Gottlieb, J.V. and Campbell, B. (2019). The Iron Ladies Revisited. *Women's History Review*, 28(2), 337–49.

Guest, C. (2017). *Becoming Feminist: Narratives and Memories*. Basingstoke: Palgrave.

Hanna, E. (2014). Contemporary Britain and the Memory of the First World War. *Matériaux pour l'histoire de notre temps*, 113–114(1), 110–17.

Hartley, L. (1980). Review of *Testament of Youth*. *Spare Rib*, 90, 48.

Herbert, H. (1982). A Radical Departure for Virago. *The Guardian*, 23 February.

Holmes, C. (2009). Obituary: Frank Cass. *Immigrants & Minorities*, 27(1), 118–22.

Hornsey, R. (2018). 'The Penguins Are Coming': Brand Mascots and Utopian Mass Consumption in Interwar Britain. *Journal of British Studies*, 57(4), 812–39.

Joannou, M. (1993). Vera Brittain's *Testament of Youth* revisited. *Literature & History*, 2(2), 46–72.

Johnson, P. (1980). Review of *The Return of the Soldier*, *The Judge* and *Harriet Hume*. *Spare Rib*, 101, 42.

Jolly, M. (2019). *Sisterhood and After: An Oral History of the Women's Liberation Movement 1968–Present*. Oxford: Oxford University Press.

Kermode, F. (1983). *The Classic: Literary Images of Permanence and Change*. Cambridge: Harvard University Press.

Khaire, M. (2017). *Culture and Commerce: The Value of Entrepreneurship in Creative Industries*. Redwood: Stanford University Press.

Kidd, J. and Sayner, J. (2018). Unthinking Remembrance? Blood Swept Lands and Seas of Red and the Significance of Centenaries. *Cultural Trends*, 27(2), 68–82.

Kovač, M., Phillips, A., van der Weel, A. and Wischenbart, R. (2017). Book Statistics. *Logos*, 28(4), 7–17.

Kuper, R. (2019). A History of Pluto Press: 50 Years of Radical Publishing. www.plutobooks.com/blog/history-pluto-press-fifty-years-radical-pub lishing/.

Marshall, A. (1983). *Changing the Word: The Printing Industry in Transition*. London: Comedia.

May, W. (2018). The Untimely Stevie Smith. *Women: A Cultural Review*, 29 (3–4), 381–97.

McCleery, A. (2002). The Return of the Publisher to Book History: The Case of Allen Lane. *Book History*, 5, 161–85.

Mitchell, K. (2010). *History and Cultural Memory in Neo-Victorian Fiction*. Basingstoke: Palgrave.

Monk, C. (2011). *Heritage Film Audiences: Period Films and Contemporary Audiences in the UK*. Edinburgh: Edinburgh University Press.

Murray, S. (2004). *Mixed Media: Feminist Presses and Publishing Politics*. London: Pluto.

Neville, G. (2017). How the Marber Grid Was Made. https://penguinser iesdesign.com/2017/02/15/how-the-marber-grid-was-made/.

No author. (1980). Guardian Diary. *The Guardian*, 3 October.

No author. (1983). London. *The Times*, 8 January.

Oakley, A. (2018). *Women: Peace and Welfare: A Suppressed History of Social Reform, 1880–1920*. Bristol: Policy Press.

Owen, U. (2019). *Single Journey Only: A Memoir*. Cromer: Salt.

Parker, R. and Sebestyen, A. (1979). A Literature of Our Own. *Spare Rib*, 78, 27–30.

Pinkerton, S. (2008). Trauma and Cure in Rebecca West's The *Return of the Soldier*. *Journal of Modern Literature*, 32(1), 1–12.

Potter, J. (2008). *Boys in Khaki, Girls in Print: Women's Literary Responses the Great War 1914–18*. Oxford: Oxford University Press.

Prestidge, J. (2019). Housewives Having a Go: Margaret Thatcher, Mary Whitehouse and the Appeal of the Right Wing Woman in

Late Twentieth-Century Britain. *Women's History Review*, 28(2), 277–96.

Purvis, J. (2013). Gendering the Historiography of the Suffragette Movement in Edwardian Britain: Some Reflections. *Women's History Review*, 22(4), 576–90.

Radway, R. (1984). *Reading the Romance*. North Carolina: University of North Carolina Press.

Riley, C. (2018). *The Virago Story: Assessing the Impact of a Feminist Publishing Phenomenon*. Oxford: Berghahn.

Robinson, D. (1982). Cinema. *The Times*, 25 May.

Robinson, D. (1983). Passionate Paradoxes. *The Times*, 7 January.

Rowbotham, S. (1972). Women's Liberation and the New Politics. In Wandor, M. ed. *The Body Politic: Writings from the Women's Liberation Movement in Britain 1969–1972*. London: Stage 1, 3–30.

Rowbotham, S. (1972). *Women, Resistance and Revolution: A History of Women and Revolution in the Modern World*. Harmondsworth: Penguin.

Rowbotham, S. (1973). *Hidden from History: 300 Years of Women's Oppression and the Fight Against It*. London: Pluto Press.

Rowbotham, S. (1990). The Beginnings of the Women's Liberation Movement in Britain. In Wandor, M. ed. *Once a Feminist: Stories of a Generation*. London: Virago, 28–43.

Samuel, R. (1992). Return to Victorian Values. *Proceedings of the British Academy*, 78, 9–29.

Samuel, R. (1994). *Theatres of Memory: Past and Present in Contemporary Culture*. London: Verso.

Scott-Brown, S. (2016). The Art of the Organiser: Raphael Samuel and the Origins of the History Workshop. *History of Education*, 45(3), 372–90.

Stevenson, G. (2019). *The Women's Liberation Movement and the Politics of Class in Britain*. London: Bloomsbury.

Stevenson, I. (2010). *Book Makers: British Publishing in the Twentieth Century*. London: British Library.

Sutherland, J.A. (1978). *Fiction and the Fiction Industry*. London: The Athlone Press.

Taylor, B. (1983). *Eve and the New Jerusalem: Socialism and Feminism in the Nineteenth Century*. London: Virago.

Thomas-Corr, J. (2020). Fiery Women. *The Sunday Times*, 23 February.

Todman, D. (2005). *The Great War: Myth and Memory*. London: Continuum.

Toye, R. (2013). From 'Consensus' to 'Common Ground': The Rhetoric of the Postwar Settlement and Its Collapse. *Journal of Contemporary History*, 48(1), 3–23.

Virago. (1993). *A Virago Keepsake to Celebrate Twenty Years of Publishing*. London: Virago.

Virago. (2019). Where Are All the Blue Plaques Celebrating Women? www.virago.co.uk/virago-news/2019/02/20/where-are-all-the-blue-plaques-celebrating-women/.

Wansell, G. (1982). Chilling View of Catholic Control. *The Times*, 14 May, 16.

Watson, N.J. ed. (2009). *Literary Tourism and Nineteenth Century Culture*. Basingstoke: Palgrave.

Weideger, P. (1988). Write On! *Ms*. July, 46–51.

Weidemann, K. (1969). *Book Jackets and Record Sleeves*. London: Thames and Hudson.

Williams, R. and Orrom, M. (1954). *Preface to Film*. London: Film Drama.

Williams, S. (1978). Preface. In *Testament of Youth*. London: Virago, 9–10.

Winship, J. (1987). *Inside Women's Magazines*. London: Pandora.

Winter, J. (2017). Commemorating Catastrophe: 100 Years On. *War & Society*, 36(4), 239–55.

Withers, D. (2015). *Feminism, Digital Culture and the Politics of Transmission: Theory, Practice and Cultural Heritage*. London: Rowman Littlefield International.

Withers, D-M. (2019). Enterprising Women: Independence, Finance and Virago Press, c.1976–93. *Twentieth Century British History*, 31(4), 479–502. https://doi.org/10.1093/tcbh/hwz044.

Withers, D-M. (2020). The Politics of the Workshop: Craft, Autonomy and Women's Liberation. *Feminist Theory*, 21(2), 217–34. https://doi.org/10.1177/1464700119859756.

Withers, D-M. (forthcoming). Virago Modern Classics: The Making of a Reprint Series. In Wilson, N., Battershill, C., Heywood, S., la Penna, D., Southworth, H., Staveley. A., Willson, E. eds. *The Edinburgh Companion to Women in Publishing, 1900–2000*. Edinburgh: Edinburgh University Press.

Wood, A. (2014). Facing Life as We Have Known it: Virginia Woolf and the Women's Co-operative Guild. *Literature & History*, 23(2), 18–34.

Woolf, V. (2012). Introductory Letter to Margaret Llewellyn Davies. In Llewellyn Davies, M. ed. *Life as We Have Known It*. London: Virago, xvi–xvii.

Cambridge Elements ≡

Publishing and Book Culture

SERIES EDITOR
Samantha Rayner
University College London

Samantha Rayner is a Reader in UCL's Department of
Information Studies. She is also Director of UCL's Centre for
Publishing, co-Director of the Bloomsbury CHAPTER
(Communication History, Authorship, Publishing, Textual
Editing and Reading) and co-editor of the Academic Book of
the Future BOOC (Book as Open Online Content) with UCL
Press.

ASSOCIATE EDITOR
Leah Tether
University of Bristol

Leah Tether is Professor of Medieval Literature and Publishing
at the University of Bristol. With an academic background in
medieval French and English literature and a professional
background in trade publishing, Leah has combined her
expertise and developed an international research profile in
book and publishing history from manuscript to digital.

ABOUT THE SERIES

This series aims to fill the demand for easily accessible, quality texts available for teaching and research in the diverse and dynamic fields of Publishing and Book Culture. Rigorously researched and peer-reviewed Elements will be published under themes, or 'Gatherings'. These Elements should be the first check point for researchers or students working on that area of publishing and book trade history and practice: we hope that, situated so logically at Cambridge University Press, where academic publishing in the UK began, it will develop to create an unrivalled space where these histories and practices can be investigated and preserved.

Cambridge Elements ≡

Publishing and Book Culture

Women, Publishing, and Book Culture

Gathering Editor: Rebecca Lyons

Rebecca Lyons is a Teaching Fellow at the University of
Bristol. She is also co-editor of the experimental BOOC (Book
as Open Online Content) at UCL Press. She teaches and
researches book and reading history, particularly female
owners and readers of Arthurian literature in fifteenth- and
sixteenth-century England, and also has research interests in
digital academic publishing.

Elements in the Gathering

Aboriginal Writers and Popular Fiction: The Literature of Anita Heiss
Fiannuala Morgan

Bluestockings and Travel Accounts: Reading, Writing and Collecting
Nataliia Voloshkova

*Virago Reprints and Modern Classics: The Timely Business of Feminist
Publishing*
D-M Withers

A full series listing is available at: www.cambridge.org/EPBC